CALIFORNIA WILDFIRE LANDSCAPING

▲▲▲▲▲▲▲▲▲▲▲▲▲▲▲▲▲▲▲▲▲▲▲▲▲▲▲▲▲▲▲▲▲▲▲▲▲▲▲

ABOUT THE AUTHOR

Maureen Gilmer has worked in virtually all aspects of horticulture and landscape design in California. In 1986, she established Professional Landscape Design, a service dedicated to the creation of fine residential landscapes. During this time she received an award for design of a Native American cultural garden for the Universtiy of California at Davis Arboretum. The author of *The Complete Guide to Northern California Gardening*, she has written extensively on the unique aesthetic of California—its history, plants, and habitats. Gilmer is a frequently featured garden writer for *Sierra Heritage* and the *Sacramento Bee*, and was a contributing editor of *Northern California Home & Garden*. Her contributing essay, "No New Ideas," appears in *New Voices: Landscape Design*, edited by Ann Lovejoy. An accomplished photographer as well as writer, Gilmer has contributed work to *Better Homes & Gardens*, *HOME*, *Fine Gardening*, *Garden Design*, *1001 Home Ideas*, *Country Living*, *Victorian Homes*, and many more. She lives in Dobbins, California.

▲▲▲▲▲▲▲▲▲▲▲▲▲▲▲▲▲▲▲▲▲▲▲▲▲▲▲▲▲▲▲▲▲▲▲▲▲▲▲

▲▲▲▲▲▲▲▲▲▲▲▲▲▲▲▲▲▲▲▲▲▲▲▲▲▲▲▲▲▲▲

California Wildfire Landscaping

Maureen Gilmer

Taylor Publishing Company
Dallas, Texas

▲▲▲▲▲▲▲▲▲▲▲▲▲▲▲▲▲▲▲▲▲▲▲▲▲▲▲▲▲▲▲

ALSO BY MAUREEN GILMER:

The Complete Guide To Northern California Gardening

Easy Lawn and Garden Care

The Complete Guide To Southern California Gardening
(*forthcoming*)

Copyright © 1994 by Maureen Gilmer

Published by Taylor Publishing Company
1550 West Mockingbird Lane
Dallas, Texas 75235

Library of Congress Cataloging-in-Publication Data

Gilmer, Maureen.
    California wildfire landscaping / Maureen Gilmer.
      p. cm.
    Includes index.
    ISBN 0-87833-864-0
    1. Firescaping—California. I. Title.
SB475.9.F57G55   1994
635.9'5—dc20   94-8523
                             CIP

Printed in the United States of America

10 9 8 7 6 5 4 3 2 1

*To the valiant fire fighters who lost their lives this summer
in the Glenwood Springs, Colorado, wildfire,
and to all the others who made the ultimate sacrifice
protecting our wildlands and homes throughout the west.*

CONTENTS

▲▲▲▲▲▲▲▲▲▲▲▲▲▲▲▲▲▲▲▲▲▲▲▲▲▲▲▲▲▲▲▲▲▲▲▲▲▲

PREFACE

There will no doubt continue to be great controversy for years to come over the problems of land management and California's growing population. New developments will see increased government regulation of subdivision planning and building locations wherever proposed residential areas interface with wild lands. Ultimately this should render these communities less vulnerable to fire in the future. But for the millions of Californians who already live in fire-prone ecosystems, we can only try to manage our own sites as prudently as possible.

The key to this book is to view the homesite in a holistic fashion. This means that no single aspect of wildfire landscaping, such as fire "resistant" plants for example, can be guaranteed to work without some attention to the other factors. In the past, information regarding all the important subjects such as native vegetation management, ornamental plants, erosion control, emergency water supply, and revegetation were supplied by different sources. As a result, it was likely that a concerned homeowner would implement only a portion of the total concept, and thus render it only marginally effective.

California Wildfire Landscaping is the first attempt to cover all the essential factors in one handbook written in language understandable to homeowners. It also deals with the aesthetic factors that are so important to residential sites, and where firescaping ordinances are in effect, it sheds some light on how to use natives as well as ornamental plants for attractive results.

But we must all keep in mind that wildfire is a dangerous and unpredictable problem, and there is no sure way to protect a home under every situation. What we *can* do is to take full advantage of every opportunity available in the hope that it will be enough to save a home.

▲▲▲▲▲▲▲▲▲▲▲▲▲▲▲▲▲▲▲▲▲▲▲▲▲▲▲▲▲▲▲▲▲▲▲▲▲

▲▲▲▲▲▲▲▲▲▲▲▲▲▲▲▲▲▲▲▲▲▲▲▲▲▲▲▲▲▲▲▲▲▲▲▲▲▲

ACKNOWLEDGMENTS

Special thanks to those who were so helpful in supplying the facts and valuable information required to write this book. Their encouragement is much appreciated.

▲ Bruce Turbeville, Fire Prevention Education Specialist, California Department of Forestry and Fire Protection, Sacramento

▲ Ernst D. Paschke, District Conservationist, USDA Soil Conservation Service

▲ Dan Smith, Director of Communications, American Forests

▲ Gerald Adams, Fire Marshall, Battalion Chief, North Lake Tahoe Fire Protection District.

▲ Tim Paysen, Riverside Forest Fire Lab

▲ Steve Arno, Intermountain Research Station, Montana

▲ Steve Kroeger, Division Chief, California Department of Forestry and Fire Protection, Oroville

▲▲▲▲▲▲▲▲▲▲▲▲▲▲▲▲▲▲▲▲▲▲▲▲▲▲▲▲▲▲▲▲▲▲▲▲▲▲

▲▲▲▲▲▲▲▲▲▲▲▲▲▲▲▲▲▲▲▲▲▲▲▲▲▲▲▲▲▲▲▲▲▲▲▲

INTRODUCTION

It's time to wake up and smell the chaparral, because sooner or later, these areas are going to burn. This is not a maybe. This is not a potential. It's genuine. It's real. It is going to happen again. The question is, when the smoke clears, will your house be standing?

> Captain Dan Young
> Orange County Fire Department
> Early November, 1993

Captain Young's words are not prophetic—they are realistic. He knows that wildland fires have always been a part of California's natural environment and they have acted in various ways to sustain and regenerate ecosystems. Some of our native plants actually have built-in mechanisms to insure they will be able to survive as a species after fires. This is not to say the plants *require* fire to reproduce as many have suggested: they simply have adapted to recurrent seasonal burns.

In some cases the entire plant may succumb, leaving only residual seed to create offspring, which can sprout in far greater numbers than if no fire had occurred at all. Take for example the lodgepole pine, a common Sierra species that produces two different types of cones. Nonserotinous cones develop and open in the same year to scatter seed on an annual basis. A second cone called serotinous matures in a similar way, but an abundance of glue-like pitch prevents its opening. These cones either remain attached to the tree indefinitely or fall to the forest floor where they are buried beneath the litter. When fire attacks an older stand of lodgepole, it melts the pitch of serotinous cones and they open with the heat. Even though every living tree in the stand may be killed

▲▲▲▲▲▲▲▲▲▲▲▲▲▲▲▲▲▲▲▲▲▲▲▲▲▲▲▲▲▲▲▲▲▲▲▲

by the fire, the following season seedlings from the serotinous cones re-populate the area. Lodgepoles have one of the fastest growing seedlings of all American conifer species.

For thousands of years seasonal fires have burned the California countryside, but they were of low intensity and rarely damaged mature plants. The ash actually improved the soil. Evidence of the recurrence of these fires has been found in growth rings of giant sequoia trees on the west slope of the Sierra, and due to the great age of these trees we have climatic records as far back as A.D. 245. Forests and other ecosystems are naturally thinned by fires so that each tree obtains enough light, water, and soil nutrients to stay healthy. The burning of seedlings reduces competition and allows older trees and shrubs to attain greater proportions.

Prior to 1850 many different California Native American tribes used fire as a land management tool. Hunting and gathering is nearly impossible in vegetation-choked areas. During the late fall or in wet winter weather the fires were lit, and would smoulder covering thousands of acres. With limited fuels and the cool moist air of winter, fires presented little damage potential to the Native Americans or wildlife.

Foresters wondered whether there were other benefits to native communities from burning besides just access and visibility. Some years ago a study was conducted on a piece of California chaparral where biologists determined the current density of deer to be about thirty per square mile. The first season after the initial controlled burn, deer populations rose to ninety-eight deer per square mile. The second year there averaged one hundred thirty-one per square mile. This sudden rise in population was attributed to the fact that burned ground tended to sprout a greater abundance of more highly nutritious grasses. This was in part stimulated by increased sunlight from shrub and tree canopy reduction. The thinning of other types of competitive seedlings further encouraged the grasses by rendering all soil moisture and nutrients available. The burning thus improved grazing for the deer, which reproduced in greater numbers, and perhaps other herds were drawn to the enriched burn sites as well. Thus the land management of the local hunting tribes proved to be highly effective in increasing their food supply.

Another more unusual example of burning by Native Americans is in the Mojave Desert at the oases where California fan palm groves have survived upon spring water for centuries. These palms retain their dead, dry fronds in a skirt of thatch that may remain on the tree for its entire life span if undisturbed. The Cahuilla tribe, which lived beneath these groves, regularly burned their palms in wet weather. Ethno-botanists studied this practice for a long time to discover exactly why the Indians continued to burn.

When asked, the Cahuilla claimed it was done to "get rid of the bugs." This refers to the giant palm-boring beetle and its destructive tunneling, which can easily kill the trees. Burning away the thatch also cleaned the trunks and made them easier to climb when harvesting the fruit stalks.

There were other reasons, for, like the deer herd increases, burning the palms encouraged prolific fruiting. A study of fan palms proved those burned within the previous four years produced about sixty per-cent more fruit. And finally, the last, but most important reason is that burning reduced competition for limited water by killing greedy cot-tonwood and willow seedlings, which also inhabit the palm oases, while leaving the palms unscathed. Here too, the selective thinning of natural vegetation shows how burning contributes to more healthy trees and forests everywhere.

But with the coming of the settlers after the Gold Rush, the Indians were discouraged from burning forests and chaparral, and naturally ig-nited fires were put out whenever possible. There are many parts of Cal-ifornia that have not burned since 1850, while before this date they were singed every few years. The litter has accumulated for nearly a century in some areas. Native plants now grow overly dense, and may be fur-ther crowded by foreign plants that have naturalized in the ecosystem, such as Scotch broom. And to complicate the threat, California receives less rain than it did in the nineteenth century, so vegetation tends to be drier and more volatile.

Take this precarious scenario and add an infestation of pine bark beetle, which is responsible for the great number of standing dead trees throughout California's forest regions. Had the forests not become so overgrown they might not be as susceptible to the beetle. Judicious pre-scribed burning or selective logging throughout the last century would have rendered the forests far more resistant to both drought and pests. And so today we are faced with a long history of neglect that has trans-formed California wildlands into hundreds of thousands of acres of tin-derbox vegetation.

Fire is a disaster grouped with floods and earthquakes as an act of God, although most wildfires are ignited by man. It is clear there will always be wildfires in this state, and encroachment of residential areas into fire-prone ecosystems creates a growing threat to people and their homes. Foresters, land managers, and fire fighting agencies across California as well as in other parts of the United States are worried by the increasing dilemma. They know it is impossible to protect homes in vulnerable terrain and heavy vegetation.

Every resident in or around fire-prone wildland must understand that informed decisions can help protect homes from this inevitable threat. If conditions remain just as they are today in California, it is a certainty that homes will burn in greater more damaging wildfires.

1

▲▲▲▲▲▲▲▲▲▲▲▲▲▲▲▲▲ ▲▲▲▲▲▲▲▲▲▲▲▲▲▲▲▲

How Vegetation and Topography Influence Wildfires

California has experienced a boom in population since World War II and is expected to continue growing at a similar rate. Our climate and diversity of ecosystems from the Pacific Coast beaches to the heights of the Sierra Nevada cannot be matched anywhere else in the United States, and as a result new residents are settling here every day. This stimulates a continual need for housing. The most desirable areas have already been developed and the growth is now reaching deeply into more rural, steep terrain. This, combined with various types of native vegetation, creates a volatile situation which not only threatens Californians but other developing parts of the United States as well. The **urban-wildland interface** is a new term being used by today's fire suppression and land management experts. It describes the increasing number of situations where residential development contacts natural ecosystems.

Fire-fighting experts would like to see more stringent controls on where development occurs in order to reduce situations that are in no way defensible, such as homes on steep hillsides where access is limited. They lament insufficient building codes concerning architecture, materials, landscaping, and management of native vegetation. Since the Oakland Hills fire, the state of California has legislated fire safety regulations that demand only the most basic vegetation controls, such as

▲▲▲▲▲▲▲▲▲▲▲▲▲▲▲▲▲▲▲▲▲▲▲▲▲▲▲▲▲▲▲▲▲▲▲

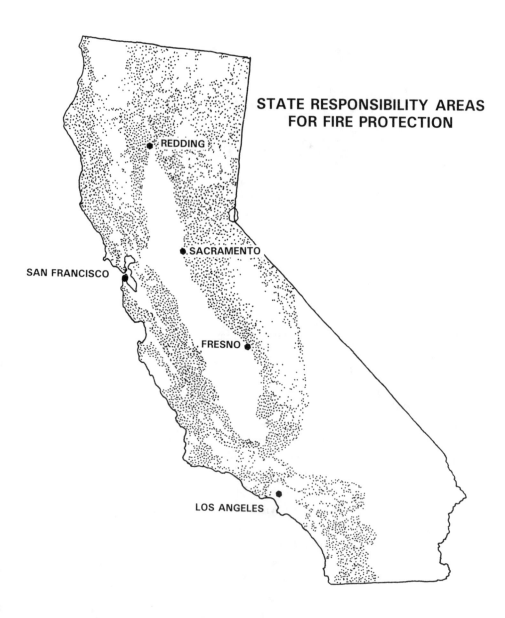

STATE RESPONSIBILITY AREAS
FOR FIRE PROTECTION

REDDING

SACRAMENTO

SAN FRANCISCO

FRESNO

LOS ANGELES

AGENCIES INCLUDED IN SRA PROTECTION:

CALIFORNIA DEPT. OF FORESTRY AND FIRE PROTECTION
U.S. FOREST SERVICE
BUREAU OF LAND MANAGEMENT
NATIONAL PARKS SERVICE

clearing fuels around homes and chimney caps. But this is just a small step, and with wildland fuels accumulating, we need to take giant leaps in establishing regulations to protect homesites.

The Nature of the Beast

All wildfires are not the same. The **behavior** of a fire is described by factors such as temperature, duration, and speed of travel. Each of these is influenced by the lay of the land, or **topography,** and the amount of vegetation, or **fuel**. When evaluating a homesite in terms of potential wildfire vulnerability, the area outside the yard or property lines is critical. This is because wildfires typically originate off site and must travel to your home, unlike a house fire, which starts within the home itself. For example, your homesite may be protected by well designed and maintained **firescape**—a defensible-space landscape. But if your next-door neighbor's house is crowded by tall weeds and overgrown chaparral shrubs, or if your property backs up to dense native vegetation, the heat and ash generated may still threaten your safety. This illustrates how important it is for entire communities to work together in reducing fire danger.

The finest example of this community effort was achieved by Neighbors for Defensible Space in the Tahoe Basin, where pine beetles and other factors have created a tremendous amount of standing dead timber. Citizens in Incline Village, Nevada, led by Fire Marshall Jerry Adams, organized the group that developed a comprehensive program of local forest management and the creation of "defensible space" around homesites. It has been highly successful and is the model for many other groups acting to reduce the overall fire danger in their communities.

Keep in mind this is no simple matter. "Neighbors" had to coordinate input, demands, and concerns from many different agencies not always in agreement with each other. It was a long and arduous effort working with the U.S. Forest Service, Tahoe Regional Planning Agency, Nevada Division of Forestry, as well as other environmental groups. Supporting the project were the North Lake Tahoe Chamber of Commerce, University of Nevada at Reno Cooperative Extension, and the North Lake Tahoe Fire District.

There are some other important terms to know which relate to the types of fuels that feed a fire.

Aerial Fuels   These consist of parts of plants located above about 5 feet from the ground, typically the canopies of trees and taller shrubs. **Crown fires** feed upon aerial fuels and travel quickly through

Homes such as these that back up to natural open spaces are the most vulnerable. Should the area be designated as habitat for endangered species, the ability to create a defensible space may be restricted by wildlife agencies responsible for enforcement of the Endangered Species Act.

tree tops until they contact shrubs or dead trees with lower fuels, which bring the flames downward to the ground.

Urban Fuels   This is a new concept that is based on fire behavior in cities. Sometimes the source is a house fire, but it can also originate from embers generated by wildland fires a long distance away. In this case rooftops act much like closely spaced trees in a forest. Roofing of closely built homes allow a fire to travel via this aerial fuel to ignite great numbers of homes as rapidly as trees in a forest fire and with similar, devastating results.

Surface Fuels   This type of fuel consists of both living and dead portions of plants from the soil level to about 4 feet high. The material lying on the ground is termed **litter**, and consists of leaves, twigs, seeds, pods, cones, and in some cases fallen trees. Surface fuels are not just restricted to wild lands. Flames can be fed by piles of lumber, household garbage, garden prunings, mounds of leaves, chaff from string trimmers, and even wood decks.

Ground Fuels   Ground fires are fed by fuels beneath the surface litter called **duff**, which often includes humus or organic matter in the soil. The greatest danger of ground fires is the fact that they can smoulder for weeks since there is insufficient oxygen to create flame. But when conditions are right, such as very low humidity or wind, they can flare up without warning. Ground fuel fires are especially dangerous *after* wildfires because they can linger unseen for long periods, then flare up when least expected.

Firestorms In many of California's most devastating fires, the term firestorm was used to describe a certain type of fire behavior. When winds, high temperatures, and speed of fire movement combine under the right conditions, a violent convection occurs. Convection is the upward movement of hot air containing smoke and embers that rises above a fire. Violent convection is this same mechanism occurring at such great intensity the fire can actually generate its own wind. As these winds increase, the fire becomes more unpredictable, with incredible power and high temperatures concentrated in a single area. It

▲▲▲

Habitat and You

California fire fighting agencies are responsible for protecting residential areas from the threat of wildfires. Historically they have reduced the threat by controlling vegetation through prescribed burning where the terrain and access made this a safe solution. They also have used goat herds to consume vegetation. Some rural homeowners in our rolling grasslands disk or cultivate the soil around their houses each year in order to turn under the dry grass before fire season.

In the last two decades, the Endangered Species Act has identified various plants and animals that are threatened with extinction due to shrinking habitat. This program has dictated that certain areas in which these species live should be preserved at any cost by simply leaving the sites untouched. As a result, efforts to burn, graze, or disk away the fire hazard have been hampered or curtailed entirely by law.

The reality of this approach to land management is that the species may be at greater risk due to neglect and other factors. For example, prescribed burns allow wildlife to move into other areas outside the fire area. Eventually they will return with the vegetation. If left untouched, this same area will burn far hotter and over such a large, uncontrolled area that the wildlife cannot escape, and plants that normally survive natural burns, such as redwood trees, will be permanently damaged or killed.

A recent example of this in the state of Virginia came to the attention of the Nature Conservancy. The Peter's Mountain mallow, a perennial wildflower, was discovered in 1927, and a group of fifty plants were the only known specimens. By 1991 only four remained. Concerned, the Nature Conservancy, Virginia Tech, and the state took action to save them. Tree rings showed an historic pattern of recurring fire for that forest, and lab tests revealed that the mallow seeds germinated far more readily after exposure to fire. Fire also reduced competition from surrounding plants with seedlings more vigorous and greedy than the mallow.

In May 1992, foresters burned a test area where the mallow once grew and after the first year new seedlings were found. The following year they conducted a second burn and about five hundred seeds germinated. Conservancy president John Sawhill said, "This shows us that simply setting aside land to protect rare or endangered species does not necessarily guarantee their protection. The remarkable comeback of Peter's Mountain mallow through the use of prescribed burning demonstrates the important role that this type of land management tool plays."

The recent burning of many of the homes in Southern California wildfires have been attributed to the elimination of fire prevention activities in favor of completely undisturbed habitat. But studies are now proving that a better way to preserve endangered species is to actively thin and burn areas where vegetation has become so overgrown. This opens up the land for predatory species and encourages a more prolific food supply. There is bound to be enormous controversy in the future over active versus passive habitat preservation, and within this dilemma resides the residential homeowner.

But there is hope that continual efforts by both fire fighting agencies and citizens will become the answer. Neighbors for Defensible Space is now the pivotal entity that assists in making the best decisions concerning their local wild lands. Perhaps other groups will soon emerge with a similar ability to balance concerns of both residents and wildlife.

▲▲

is easy to see why firestorm conditions have been responsible for many fire fighter deaths in the past.

Fire and Topography

One seasoned fire fighter says that fire moves on the land like water—but in reverse. For example, water runs down a slope, but fire tends to move upward. Where water flows down the sides of a canyon to collect at the bottom in a concentrated stream, fire conversely gathers strength in the low parts of a canyon and rages up the sides. Use this water analogy to visualize how fire is likely to behave in the topography around your homesite.

Hot air always travels upward. Fires originating at the base of a slope tend to move quickly upward because heat is always rising, and on hills this is where unburned fuel is closest to the flames. The steeper the hill, the faster the fire travels. The rising heat actually preheats and dries out the foliage of plants so they ignite far more easily than when fire is moving down slope. If a home is located part way up the hill, it is practically impossible to defend in the blast furnace of rising heat and flame.

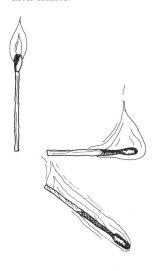

Using a Match to Understand Fire Behavior

You can use wood kitchen matches to get a better idea of how fire behaves on sloping ground. Strike the first match and hold it upright as shown and note how long it takes for the flame to reach your fingers. Dispose of the burned match safely. Strike a second match and hold it in a horizontal position to see how this angle increases the speed of the flame. The third match angle downward and you'll discover how rapidly it burns. This third position is the situation of steep slopes with the fuel preheating the vegetation or structures.

Miraculously this home escaped damage from the fire that moved up the canyon. Slopes below homes on the left lacked dense vegetation, which clearly slowed the fire and saved them as well.

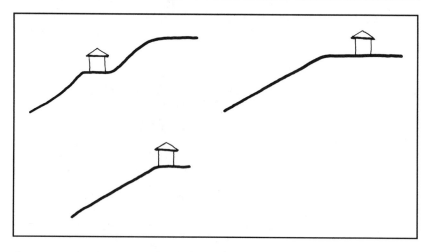

Structure Positions on Slopes

Most homes on steep terrain fit into one of these three scenarios. **Upper left:** *This danger-ous, cut-and-fill lot is highly vulnerable, as there is likely to be fuel both above and below the building. There is very little room around the building for defense, and heat radiating off the back slope through windows of the house will ignite interior fuels.* **Lower left:** *a house perched on the edge of a hill is preheated by the time intense flames reach the top of the slope. There is no space on the slope side of the house for fire fighters or their equipment.* **Right:** *This house still enjoys a hilltop view but is set back from the top of the slope. This pulls the building out of the direct path of rising heat and flame and provides plenty of room for fire fighters to defend the site.*

"Cliff-hanger" homes perched on the tops of slopes are usually built to take advantage of an unobstructed view. Sometimes portions of the building or attached decking actually jut out from the hill top. These homes are vulnerable in two ways. First, the sheer drop on one or more sides of the building prevents access for fire fighters. Second, the house sits directly in the path of the flames, and as the fire moves up the slope the rising heat will literally cook the building while bathing it in a rain of embers well before the fire contacts the flamm-able materials.

One exception to this was illustrated by a single house built in this vulnerable position but left literally unscathed in a Laguna Beach neigh-borhood where the surrounding homes were burned to the ground. It sat perched on the edge of a very steep slope but the owner, both archi-tect and engineer, designed the house with all known fire-resistant qualities. He also planted a fire resistant green belt around the house. His efforts were so successful that the house has become a landmark, proving the theories of fire conscious materials and design can some-times overcome less defensible topography.

FIRESCAPING TIP

▲ Experienced fire fighters believe that wind often influences fire behavior more than topography. In fire season, Southern California's Santa Anas and Northern California's north winds are two of the most serious fire driving winds. They also contribute to dreaded firestorms. When reviewing topography of your homesite or a future homesite, be sure to consider the direction of these winds during the dry fire season for a more accurate picture of vulnerability.

▲ South- and west-facing slopes tend to be more fire prone than those looking north or east. This is because grasses turn brown earlier in the year on these exposures, which extends their fire season. Shrubs and trees also experience greater soil moisture evaporation and higher summer temperatures. Statistics prove that south- and west-facing slopes do experience a higher incidence of fire ignition and burn at greater intensities.

The slopes below these houses are about as steep as they get. Winds must have had an influence on why some of these houses burned and others didn't. Every one of these houses is too close to the cliffs, a situation that subjects them to direct heat of convection columns rising before the flames. These houses are very difficult and dangerous for fire fighters to defend as access to all sides of the house is limited.

13

A house located on top of the hill but set well back from the edge of a slope is in a better position, but only if it is separated from surrounding vegetation by open space. This breaks the continuity of the fire and creates defensible space, although defense against an intense burn may be virtually hopeless as temperatures reach incredible levels. Fire lines are often drawn on the tops of these ridges to stop flames as they lose momentum before descending the other side of the hill.

Many of our most devastating fires have originated in canyons such as Laguna, Malibu, and Topanga canyons of Southern California. These canyons are narrow, with steep, high walls. This arrangement acts much like a chimney, drafting the flames up one or both walls at the same time. In wider canyons the fire may travel up one side, then jump across to the other side when embers are driven by the wind. A canyon with both walls blazing becomes incredibly hot, with intensity much greater than in any other fire situation.

California's Most Fire-prone Ecosystems

Fire-prone ecosystems contain large amounts of fuel to feed a wildfire and are typically located in rolling hills or steep mountainous terrain. The greater amount of fuel provided by plants in the ecosystem, the hotter and more aggressive the fire. Most urban-wildland or rural homesites fall into one of these three conditions, which should influence the way you view the threat of fire and how you must act to reduce it.

The number of standing dead trees in this ruin suggests this was once a beautiful, tree-covered homesite. This home had many liabilities: 1. steep terrain for limited access, 2. mid-slope location with fuel both above and below house, 3. abundance of available conifer fuels.

The town of Laguna Beach had only two escape routes, Coast Highway and Laguna Canyon. The fire started in this canyon, developed speed and intensity in this narrow area, and completely blocked evacuation. This forced all traffic to use Coast Highway, which had only one lane in each direction. Fire victims tell of gridlock that prevented their escaping the town as flames raged all around them. In many California communities, particularly those along the coast, access may be limited to just a few thoroughfares, which must be shared with fire fighting trucks and equipment. When traffic jams or gridlock occurs, fire fighters cannot reach the fire and residents going the opposite direction cannot escape it.

Oak Woodland

Early explorers of coastal California were amazed by the infinite rolling grasslands, verdant green in spring, then blonde- or wheat-colored in the late summer. In areas of sufficient ground water there were groves of oak trees of various species, some massive like the valley oak (*Quercus lobata*) and others evergreen such as live oaks (*Quercus agrifolia*). The land was described as parklike and the large-scale cattle and sheep ranches took advantage of this endless natural pasture.

Although not technically woodland, another type of vegetation, the coastal scrub, often blends into oak woodlands so subtly that the change in plant communities goes unnoticed. This landscape also contains grasses and bears a strong resemblance to those plant communities bordering the inland deserts. There, tufts of low-growing sagebrush and yucca comprise the most visible shrubs and perennials.

What oak woodland and scrub ecosystems have in common is limited fuel. Dry grasses ignite very quickly, then the flame lasts but a few moments and moves on. Sagebrush may burn longer, but low-growth habits tend to limit fuel volumes. A fire in grasslands moves so rapidly

California's grassy oak woodland ecosystem.

it can be difficult for fire fighters to keep up with the flames. Fast-moving fires tend to burn at lower temperatures and the soil cools more quickly after the flames pass.

Firescaping in grasslands is much easier than in other plant communities because the uncultivated areas may be either grazed, mowed,

Grassland fires move very quickly but a fireline may be drawn at any sizeable road.

or disked, all of which practically eliminate fuel availability. If a grass-land fire approaches your homesite, there is less potential to ignite the ornamental plants in green belts because flames in grass tend to be shorter in stature and burn for a limited time. Only if there is an abundance of native trees or shrubs does the heat and intensity of these fires increase.

Chaparral

This unique and extremely volatile ecosystem occurs only in Arizona and California at elevations from about one thousand feet up to four thousand feet, although this varies depending on location relative to mountain ranges and exposures. It consists of a mixture of plant species including trees, shrubs, and perennials, all of which tend to be woody in nature and tolerant of the long dry summers and rugged terrain of the foothills. Trees include both evergreen and deciduous oaks, Digger pines, and madrone.

Chaparral is made notorious by the shrubs which are some of our most beautiful native landscape plants. But it is these oily, combustible, densely growing shrubs that make fire fighting in chaparral areas incredibly difficult. Not only is it highly volatile, chaparral tends to be so heavily vegetated with large, stiff plants, fire fighters find it difficult to move around freely.

Parts of northern California were logged in the early twentieth century. The shrubs and scrub trees grew to create the tangled mess shown here, which is a common site in many foothill areas throughout the state. This situation is not only difficult to clear, but becomes inaccessible to fire fighters.

It is this ecosystem that the California Native Americans sought to keep open by annual burning. Frequent burns reduced the number of seedlings and allowed older individuals to grow unencumbered by competition for what little moisture and nutrients that were contained in sloping foothill soils. Many of these shrubs, such as manzanita and ceanothus, have evolved to survive periodic fires by sprouting from stumps, and seed germination increases after exposure to flame.

After California development began to encroach into chaparral ecosystems, all burning by Native Americans ceased. What logging occurred allowed vast areas to regrow with nothing but dense stands of shrubs, typically manzanita. A typical acre of unburned chaparral today may be timbered with bushy scrub oaks and manzanita shrubs that grow to fifteen feet high if left untouched. Patches of poison oak, California lilac (*Ceanothus* spp.), and Christmas berry (*Heteromeles arbutifolia*) choke the ground plane, preventing larger forms of wildlife from penetrating these thickets. Where burning once killed off the majority of new seedlings, they are now surviving and filling in the gaps wherever possible. This reduces the amount of soil moisture and nutrients for the older plants and as a result they all become overly dry and stressed during summer.

In chaparral there is no need for ladder fuels. Most of the plants grow with foliage nearly to the ground so that when fire strikes, the entire plant is engulfed at once. Many chaparral species contain unusually high amounts of volatile oils that are part of the plants' ability to survive long dry summers. Manzanita wood has long been valued for its density and heating value, and early California blacksmiths used it as a substitute for coal.

Imagine steep rolling hills literally blanketed with chaparral vegetation. During the summer, plants dry out and become partially dormant to survive the hot, rainless months. Their moisture content becomes extremely low during prolonged droughts. When fire hits the dense growth of chaparral during the dry winds of late summer and fall, it literally explodes into flame, and since plants here may be twenty feet or more in height, they fuel very tall flames that burn at extremely hot temperatures. The plants also continue burning for quite some time after the first flames move through the stand because of the fuel load.

Chaparral fires are some of our most devastating for the following reasons.

1. Topography is usually steep and rolling.
2. Fuel loads are extremely high due to density of vegetation.

3. Fire burns longer and hotter than grass fires.
4. Roadways (or lack of them) in chaparral belts often limit access.
5. Houses tend to be built for views which makes them difficult to defend due to hillside and ridgetop locations.
6. Much of California's foothill regions are natural chaparral areas, or became so after logging.

Forests

California forests tend to occur in two basic types. The inland forests of the Sierra and other ranges consist of different pines, aspen, and oaks, which are all capable of surviving extreme cold and very arid, infertile conditions. Along the northwestern coast are the more moist redwood forests, which include tan oak, fir, redwoods, and bay. These coastal areas receive more rain and may contain patches of dense understory vegetation such as huckleberry, California lilac, and rhododendron. Due to the higher amounts of rainfall and humidity, redwood forests are less combustible but still burn with great intensity during fire season and drought.

Over the years the no-burn policy of forest agencies has combined with logging and other factors to change the nature of forests in California as well as many other parts of the United States. The result of thousands of years of evolution is a delicate balance between species to make the forest more capable of surviving under extreme conditions. But when altered, this ecosystem loses some of its natural survival mechanisms.

The most well-documented situation is in the Lake Tahoe region, where original forests consisted primarily of open stands of more drought-resistant ponderosa, Jeffrey, and sugar pines, while moisture-loving white fir remained clustered in the canyons and on shady north slopes. Regular burns by Native American tribes and lightning fires helped to retain this optimum density of trees. But with the Gold Rush on the west slope Mother Lode, and the silver mines of Nevada's Comstock Lode, there was suddenly great demand for timber. The Sierra Nevada was subsequently logged to supply wood for mine shoring, railroad ties, fuel, and building materials. Only the inferior white fir was left behind. As a result, the current forest in the Tahoe Basin was seeded by the cones of white fir and now this is the dominant tree. But being moisture loving it does not fare well during times of drought and its subsequent weakened condition has invited the pine bark beetle invasions.

Destruction of trees by pine bark beetles is not restricted to the Tahoe Basin. It is killing trees throughout the forested portions of the state, particularly in more arid inland regions. Our forests have become overgrown with seedlings blanketing every inch of open space. In the past they would be burned off by the Indians or lightning fires if left untouched, and the forest would thin itself. But today what little light, nutrients, and water is available must be shared by far too many individuals. As a result, those less capable will become stressed and allow entry of the bark beetles and other opportunistic parasites.

The ideal solution to this problem is to implement programs of selective logging and prescribed burning. Unfortunately, foresters are prevented from both of these mitigation measures by environmental restrictions, habitat preservation, and other public concerns. The general belief is to leave the forests untouched, but the reality is that they have already been altered. In theory this means of habitat preservation may seem like a wise decision, but in fact it has actually contributed to forest decline. If involved in a wildfire today, the forests will burn so intensely that even the fire-resistant species will have no chance of survival.

Homes located within these forests are vulnerable to crown fires, which travel through the tops of trees and move very quickly. When it drops to the ground the fire feeds upon the accumulations of litter, dead twigs, branches, and leaves. If there is sufficient litter, the organic matter within the soil may burn and the elusive ground fire will begin to smoulder and literally sterilize the earth by consuming nutrient-rich duff.

The sight of a fifty-foot pine tree fully engulfed in flame is a humbling experience. Imagine the survival prospects of a home only twenty feet tall surrounded by dozens of flaming pines, the radiant heat so great the air is no longer breathable. If the pine needle litter is also burning, the flames move quickly to the structure, consuming all combustible material in its path.

Many of these forests are in steep terrain, far from civilization, with the only hope of containment being aerial bombardment. But even then fire fighters know it is often mother nature who ultimately decides where and when the fire is stopped. Isolated home sites, narrow winding roads, and low populations reduce the ability to fight forest fires. This illustrates how essential it is for residents within our California forest lands to create their own defensible space if there is to be any chance of saving the home.

Urban Forests

As the Berkeley Hills fire proved in 1991, there are other sorts of wildfires that are not related to native ecosystems. During this devastating fire, homes clustered in well-populated areas burned because the structures and the surrounding landscaping provided sufficient fuel to create a crown fire condition. The wind and other factors contributed to a firestorm that raged through the homes at an incredible rate. There was little hope of putting out such a fire, driven by relentless dry winds into tinder-dry, drought-stricken landscapes. This control problem was compounded by the fact that the Berkeley Hills are accessed by a series of narrow, winding streets that traversed some very steep slopes.

Researcher Tim Payson of the Riverside Forest Fire Lab feels strongly that the urban forest fire presents nearly as great a hazard as fires in wild lands. Imagine an urban neighborhood of single-family dwellings closely spaced and surrounded by dehydrated landscape trees. In older communities the roofing material may be wood shingles or shakes, which ignite easily and develop crown fire conditions. Add stepping stones of drought-desicated landscape trees between houses and you have the worst fuel-loading conditions of a forest or chaparral fire.

This urban forest fire is not restricted to wood-roofed houses. One fire fighter watched sparks lodge in the open ends of tile roofs to begin burning the homes around the eaves. In older neighborhoods where vegetation has matured, as in Berkeley, our California droughts and hot late summer winds create a deadly situation wherever you live. This shows that increased consciousness of our very real fire threat here in California must be realized by both rural and urban dwellers alike.

Laguna Fire, 1993. Note density of hillside homes in background similar to those burned.

Your Home and Homesite: Selection, Structures, and Insurance

The California Department of Forestry believes our state contains "the most severe wildfire conditions in the world!" With increased urban-wildland contact from development in grasslands, chaparral, and forest areas, the question is not will it burn, but when.

Accepting the fact that all homes will be threatened by fire at one time or another, those with greatest chances of survival must be properly located, constructed of resistant materials, and on a site naturally suitable for creating defensible space. **Defensible space** is defined as a managed area around a home with limited fuel availability, which helps to reduce the intensity and speed of a fire. It also provides a place for fire fighters to take a stand when protecting your house. Homes or homesites that cannot meet this criteria are not a good investment in California.

Regardless of how much homeowner's fire insurance you carry, there is no amount of money that will make up for the losses of a lifetime—the baby pictures, the clock your grandfather made, the family heirloom silver. Those who dismiss the threat of fire because of sizeable insurance policies are playing a dangerous game. For there is always the more serious threat, as in the Berkeley fire, that someone may be injured or killed, a loss that no insurance policy will compensate.

▲▲▲

Hunting Down a Defensible Homesite

The best way to protect yourself against a vulnerable homesite is to avoid purchasing one. A vast number of new and resale homes in California are at great risk of fire. The more rural the site, the greater potential of wildfire. But if you know what to look for in a bare lot or home, you will be able to sort through the properties to find the most defensible one.

New subdivisions are typically created from a larger tract of land. The lots of the subdivision may range in size from a city lot to small ranches of numerous acres. In many fire-conscious areas, cities and county planning departments are requiring these subdivisions provide adequate access for fire fighting equipment and demand there be water hydrants at various points within the development. Some areas even require each homesite to store a designated amount of water and a delivery system that ties into interior ceiling sprinklers.

But most rural parts of California do not have these requirements with their subdivision planning process, and in this case each homesite relies on its own domestic well for water. Some of these wells produce as little as two gallons per minute, hardly sufficient for even daily household needs much less fire protection. Without a community water source, there is rarely a close, accessible water supply for fire fighting efforts in dry parts of the state. When house or property hunting, always keep this water availability issue in mind.

Fire fighting agencies vary according to where you live. In the most rural areas, such as the extreme northern Sierra Nevada and other mountain ranges, there is only the California Department of Forestry and Fire Protection, with stations widely distributed in remote areas. The CDF's primary responsibility is to control wildland fires and keep them *away* from residential areas or single isolated homes. CDF also responds to the scene of a structure fire along with volunteer or local fire departments in order to prevent the flames from igniting surrounding vegetation. If the flames do jump into the surrounding grass, chaparral or forest, the fire fighters will need every drop in their tanks to prevent a major disaster.

In rural areas the role of fighting structure fires falls to the county fire fighting agencies, and in many cases it is the local volunteer fire department. This is made up of citizens who volunteer their efforts to fight fires because local government agencies cannot provide a full-time station close enough to their communities to reach a fire in time. But despite the efforts of these valiant volunteers, precious time is lost because they must be notified of the fire, drive to the fire station, and then reach the home or property with their equipment. It's easy to see this is not the

FIRESCAPING TIP

It's easy to see how essential it is for *you* the homeowner to have some means of fighting your own fires. By the time a fire fighter reaches your home, chances are it will already be engulfed in flames. A fire-safe homesite and building is the best way to prevent a house fire, or ignition from a wildfire. To fight either structure or wildland fires yourself, a private water supply and the proper fire fighting equipment are the best investments you will ever make.

most expedient fire fighting arrangement, but it is better than the alternative—none at all. (However, insurance rates may be higher for areas served only by volunteer fire departments.)

When looking for a home in a new area, inquire at the nearest fire station about its capability, and whether it is permanently staffed or volunteer. Note how far the station is from your home and the conditions of the roadways in route. Don't forget that fires sometimes occur in the winter too, when snow or mud may complicate access. Find out where the nearest California Department of Forestry station is from the homesite as well. But remember, it may be only staffed during the summer months.

Qualities of a Defensible Homesite

1. Topography

Avoid homes or lots on hillsides or steep cut-and-fill sloping subdivisions. Fire tends to burn more quickly on hillsides, and these sites are more difficult for fire fighters to surround and protect from oncoming flames. Deep canyons, particularly if choked with vegetation, are equally as risky, with even greater difficulty for access than on slopes. You should be able to clear and manage an area at least one hundred feet on all sides of your home and hopefully not be dependent on your neighbor's attention to clearing for the safety of your homesite. Some homesites are so difficult to defend that insurance companies may now be reluctant, or even refuse, to write a policy for them.

2. Wildland Interface

Avoid homes adjacent to open space that cannot be managed to reduce fire danger. For example, the residents of Laguna Beach were sub-

Although it is a view lot, this home is still standing because it was set back from the edge of the slope with plenty of access on all sides for fire fighters and their equipment. It is constructed of stucco with a tile roof, and probably has double-paned windows. There are also no trees close to the building, and virtually none on the sloping sides either.

jected to greater hazards due to the restrictions by wildlife agencies on grazing or prescribed burning of open-space "habitat." One way to find out is to obtain the Environmental Impact Report for the subdivision through the local planning department and read the biology reports it contains. But where older subdivisions are concerned, the EIR may not exist or be outdated. You may also contact the California Department of Fish and Game or the U.S. Fish and Wildlife Service for their reports on the surrounding area and whether it is currently considered habitat for an endangered species or likely to become so in the future.

3. Access

Road and street networks, whether public or private, unless exempted, shall provide for safe access for emergency wildland fire equipment and civilian evacuation concurrently, and shall provide unobstructed traffic circulation during a wildfire emergency.

Sections 1273.00 through 1273.11
California Board of Forestry
State Responsibility Area Fire-safe Regulations

Many rural communities have a network of poorly signed roads, some paved, others just gravel. The unpaved roads can be county maintained, but some subdivisions share communal private roads maintained by the residents it serves as a group. Homeowner's associations of this sort can be rife with disagreement, particularly when they discover how expensive it is to keep a road in good shape. Road maintenance requires regular grading with heavy equipment, addition of road-base gravel, and reconstruction of drainage features that prevent wash-outs and pot holes.

When culverts and bridges are involved, it can really get sticky. A bridge capable of supporting fire fighting trucks must be built to withstand at least forty thousand pounds of weight. If one or more of the group refuse to contribute their share to the road maintenance work, the others may be forced to make up the difference.

Access also relates to the width of the road or your own driveway. Some rural driveways can be unusually long or steep as they are not governed by roadway construction limits established by either California Department of Transportation, the county, or city. Sharp curves may be impossible for fire trucks to maneuver. Over time, natural vegetation

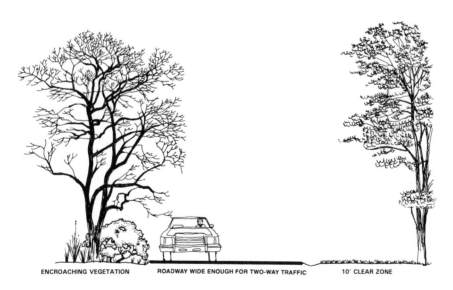

ENCROACHING VEGETATION   ROADWAY WIDE ENOUGH FOR TWO-WAY TRAFFIC   10' CLEAR ZONE

Road or Driveway Cross Section

A typical road lane is 12 feet across, a two-way road at least 24 feet across. Unless there are cliffs or slopes on the immediate road shoulder, a rural roadway can be narrower, but only as long as there is room to pass an oncoming car or fire truck by using that extra space. Treatment of the vegetation adjacent to the road is essential if it is to remain open when a fire sweeps through. If the vegetation shown on the left side was to be similar on the opposite side of the road, it could become a tunnel of fire. The 10-foot clear zone shown on the right is a minimum, and if an even greater area can be cleared, the access will be safer.

may narrow the shoulders of the road and although your car may have no difficulty managing, the fire fighting trucks could be prevented from entering. Also, imagine a driveway with encroaching vegetation totally aflame on both sides. This picture does not make evacuation or access by fire fighters seem possible. Think long and hard about the work required to clear brush for ten feet on either side of your private road or five feet for a driveway every year that you own the home

Yet another issue which frequently confronts fire fighters is the single-lane driveway. If an evacuating family is exiting through this conduit, the fire fighters heading toward the flames will meet the other vehicle head on, and will have to back down the road until it is wide enough to pass, then go forward again. This delay might be just long enough to prevent them from saving your house.

Rural residents often joke about the convoluted directions to find a house in isolated hill communities. "Turn left at the third tree after the red reflector just 1.3 miles off the main road," is an example of what it takes to find some of these places. Fire fighters have an equally hard time finding your house under these conditions without clear road signs and address numbers. Most people make the mistake of never learning their street address when there is no rural mail delivery. The number of your house and that of your neighbors' helps police and fire fighters to find your home in case of emergency. Be sure it is prominently displayed.

4. Emergency Water

Water is a scarce commodity in many parts of California, but it is essential if you are to be able to fight fires at your rural home. Of course, in communities with built-in fire water systems you need not be as concerned about this factor, unless the hydrant is a long distance from your homesite. There is plenty more in chapter 4 on this subject, but for now it is sufficient to know that a homesite that has its own water supply and storage system is a thousand times more valuable than one that does not.

Natural sources include springs and streams, but be sure to evaluate their output or levels during the late summer and fall when some may dry up completely. Remember this is the time of year that water is the most needed. Ponds or swimming pools are other good water reservoirs, but pond water levels may fluctuate depending on whether they are fed by streams or springs. Domestic wells are rated by their gallons per minute, and low output cannot be relied upon because some will become exhausted during prolonged droughts, or if pumped constantly over long periods. Limited supply can be compensated for by swimming pools or large water tanks, but both are expensive to buy and install. Think long and hard about this feature of your new or existing site, because a dry home is likely to become a burned home.

Buildings and Materials

A house may be able to better resist nearby wildland fires if it is constructed properly. This relates primarily to roofing, but there are other factors such as design which also contribute to this ability to deter ignition. The major offender in every case is the wood shake or shingle roof. Older neighborhoods may have many homes with this kind of roofing; some newer communities strictly forbid them. If your home has shingles on the sides or roof, consider it highly vulnerable to fire, and even though the material may have been treated to make it less flammable, this chemical will gradually disappear after just a few years.

Roof material has a lot do with a defensible home. Many fire insurance companies require roofing Class C or better before they write a policy. However, future legislation may change these requirements, so check local and state building codes. Roofing materials are rated as follows:

Class A Maximum Protection
Clay tiles, concrete tiles, fiberglass shingles, metal tiles, perlite shakes, class-a-rated pressure-treated cedar shakes, built-up roof (9 layers fiberglass).

Class B Moderate Protection
Class-b-rated pressure-treated cedar shakes, metal tiles, built-up roof (7 layers).

Class C Minimum Protection
Asphalt shingles, built-up roof (3 layers), class-c pressure-treated cedar shakes.

Non-Rated
Avoid any roofing materials with less than a Class C rating and those that have no rating.

The siding of your house is another potentially combustible material. Views of the Laguna fire damage show large sheets of stucco siding still intact, while the roofs and studs that surrounded them were burned to ashes. Stucco and masonry are always better than wood siding. The thicker these materials are applied, the less heat they absorb and the greater the insulation factor.

FIRESCAPING TIP

Although your home may be roofed with a Class A rated material, its effectiveness may be influenced by how well sealed the edges are. Sparks and embers tend to lodge in nooks and crannies of roofing. Tile roofs often have openings at the ends just above the fascia or rain gutters. Roofs of this type have been known to ignite and burn beneath the tiles from embers that entered through these openings. Fire experts insist these be closed off with suitable material.

Spray-on Treatments—What Fire Chiefs Say

The California Fire Chiefs Association feels there is some confusion as to the effectiveness of spray-on treatments for wood roofing. Unscrupulous contractors may not always be truthful about every factor of their products. Consider the following facts:

1. No spray-on application has passed standard tests recognized by the fire and building code agencies, nor has it been approved by the state fire marshal. Demand copies of test results from Underwriter's Laboratories or building code agencies if indicated by seller.
2. Flame-spread ratings and treatments are applicable only to materials used in the *interior* of buildings.
3. Guarantees usually do not assure fire resistance but refer to a re-spray if material fails (a lot of good that is with no house left).
4. Cleaning the roof prior to application may cause cracking of shakes and shingles from foot traffic or water pressure from equipment. *Replacement* of wood roofs with Class A materials is the only means of reducing hazard.

Vents that allow air exchange in attics and crawl spaces also make the house vulnerable. Sparks enter attics through these openings, or through foundation ventilation openings, to ignite the beams and materials beneath your floors. The more vents, as well as other nooks and crannies in the architecture, the greater opportunity there is for an ember to lodge and ignite the materials around it. It is recommended that all vents be covered with a non-flammable ¼-inch mesh screen.

The fire ignited the roof of this house and the flames spread throughout the interior, consuming all the wood structure. All that is left is the exterior wall stucco, which crumbled when its support burned.

Windows can also transmit heat from outdoor flames into the house, particularly if they are facing hillsides or masses of vegetation that burn unusually hot. The larger the window the greater the danger. Drapes and furnishings inside the house can actually catch fire through single-pane windows. Double-pane windows are recommended for a more fire resistant home. They have greater insulating qualities and are less subject to breaking when exposed to high temperatures.

Another vulnerable part of the house is the eaves. Open eaves that leave the ends of roof joists exposed are thin and become hot very quickly. Embers rising from burning vegetation around the house tend to gather underneath them. All eaves should be no deeper than absolutely necessary, which may conflict with some of the solar-heat calculations required by building departments for greater energy efficiency. To comply with building codes, box in the eaves. Regardless of the scale of existing or proposed eaves, they should always be tightly boxed in with fire-resistant materials.

Insurance

In the past, some California homeowners purposefully undervalued their homes when buying fire insurance to lower the premiums. Although they may have saved a few dollars each month, many people found this was penny wise and pound foolish after their houses burned to the ground in the latest Laguna Beach fire. Afterwards they discovered there was no hope of building a new house with the limited amount paid by the insurance company.

If these homeowners had approached the problem of cost in more logical terms, they might have discovered that increasing the deductible may have saved just as much money. For example, an annual premium with a $100 deductible may cost roughly double that of the same coverage with a $2500 deductible. It is the total devastation of a home that few can recover from on their own; the first few thousand dollars of damage can be resolved by personal loans or payment plans. Therefore, it is far wiser to reduce insurance premiums by raising the deductible than undervaluing the house.

But the problem of being underinsured is usually unknown to the homeowner for a variety of reasons. Perhaps the most common is that California real estate during the last two decades has skyrocketed in value, particularly prime lots in affluent communities or along the ocean front. A second factor is that new home construction is subjected to far more costly regulations today than in the past. For example, insulation, roofing, window type and quantity, heating and air conditioning are all more expensive to install, not due to inflation, but because of building department standards.

In the event your home does burn, it's essential you carry sufficient fire insurance with a policy that covers a number of important factors. If you already have a policy, review it and make appropriate adjustments in order to be sure you are adequately covered. And every year that the policy is renewed, review it again just to be sure you are not left underinsured in the event of disaster.

Important Factors to Consider When Buying Fire Insurance

1. Replacement Costs

If you purchased your home twenty years ago for $100,000, chances are your insurance policy was written to provide a replacement value of that amount. But if you're lucky, today the same home may be worth $250,000. It's easy to see that a policy must be updated as property values rise in order to provide an accurate replacement value. Everyone should look at his or her policy and determine what that amount actually is. If it is lower than the home's current value, which can be estimated by your insurance agent, then you should increase your policy limits. Be sure to make adjustments for improvements such as installation of a swimming pool, deck, or remodeling.

2. Building Standards

Today's city and county building departments are growing more strict about construction methods and materials allowed in home building. Energy regulations restrict the number, size, and type of windows. They may also dictate the efficiency rating of air conditioning and heating units as well as insulation. Where there was once no criteria regarding roofing material, there may now be only Class A allowed in your neighborhood. There can also be more subtle changes in the Uniform Building Code, which add nickel-and-dime costs to the price of a new house. Put them all together and you discover replacement cost applies not only to inflation, but to the rising price of conforming to regulations and codes.

3. Personal Possessions

Insurance policies cover not only the building, but its contents as well. Police departments recommend homeowners document their possessions in the event of burglary, but this is also a good idea in case of fire. Furniture, audiovisual equipment, computers, and anything else of value is worth documenting with a home video camera or still photos. Take the information to your insurance agent and discuss whether the "personal contents" section of your policy adequately covers these items. Special policies are available for fine art, jewelry, furs, or rare antiques. For smaller items a fire-resistant box or safe may keep them more accessible than a bank safe deposit box, and for less money than an insurance policy.

Homeowner's policies don't always cover home offices, which may contain costly high-tech equipment, records, and files that may be impossible to replace. The losses may completely destroy the business. For adequate coverage take out a small business owner's policy that includes liability coverage.

4. Living Expenses

We all have a tendency to file away our policies without ever having read all the details. One aspect of a home fire policy is that it provides money to cover living expenses until you find a new home. This is a finite amount, and if you plan to rebuild it may be a year or longer before you can move into the new house. Find out exactly what your policy provides for living expenses, and if you think more coverage would be needed, discuss this with your agent. Remember, if your house burns to the ground, as most do in wildfire scenarios, you will be left with little or nothing. Getting back on your feet may be overwhelmingly expensive.

5. Site Improvements

Insurance policies covering city homes are fairly straightforward, but when it comes to rural properties there are other things to be considered. Wildfires burn more than just homes; they destroy fencing, irrigation systems, outbuildings, garden or farm equipment, and unfortunately livestock too. There is a difference in price, as well as coverage, between farm or ranch insurance policies and those strictly for homes.

If your home is rural but not a working farm or ranch, it is wise to discuss any site improvements with your agent to find out if they are covered. For example, if you have recreational horses and a stable that may contain expensive tack and equipment, it would be difficult to replace yourself if burned by a wildfire and not covered by your insurance policy. It is a good idea to buy an additional endorsement for these items as well as the horses if they are expensive show-quality animals. This also applies to fencing, especially if decorative, because replacement may be *very* expensive, particularly on a large scale. Other rural improvements that should be covered in your policy include domestic well house and equipment, sheds, barns, outdoor electrical lines/lighting, and irrigation systems.

▲▲

Understanding Insurance Terms

Guaranteed replacement cost   Replacement cost is based on a fixed amount dictated by the policy, and provides no additional funds under any circumstances. Guaranteed replacement is more open-ended and will cover your property even if it exceeds the policy limit. Understandably, this type of coverage costs you higher premiums.

Inflation-guard clause   This clause assures you the policy is readjusted each year upon renewal to cover increases in local construction costs. It factors in both changes in building standards and inflation rates.

Actual cash value   This figure is calculated by insurance companies by factoring in depreciation in finding the value of your house.

Endorsement   If there is additional coverage over and above the basic policy, an endorsement of the terms will be attached to the main policy. This is where you will find specialized coverage of high-tech equipment, art, antiques, or jewelry, as well as many other unusual items of value.

▲▲

Farm and ranch policies are designed to cover these things as well as the farmer's commodities such as orchards, stored feed, haystacks, general livestock, tack, farming equipment, large barns, and harvested crops. Special endorsements may apply to purebred livestock such as a breeding bull or stallion, which may be valued at tens of thousands of dollars. The insurance agent will require a value assessment of items to be covered, then write the policy based on this information.

Homes in this community would not rate well in an insurance evaluation. Homes are predominantly shingle roofs. Trees are a mix of eucalyptus, California pepper, and pines, all volatile species. Tree canopies overlap, creating opportunity for crown fires. Homesites cluster in a low canyon where fire intensity can build.

How Insurance Companies Rate Fire Danger

Insurance companies use a safety rating system to establish the fire insurance premium of homes in suburban or rural areas. It takes into consideration surrounding vegetation, topography, housing density, fire history, water availability, and local ordinances, all factors relating to the vulnerability of a home or homesite. Since the state fire safety regulations go into effect next year, any insurance companies that are not using the system now are likely to adopt it soon. Consider these issues when evaluating an existing home or preparing to buy a new one.

In this system, the lower the total score, the safer the homesite. A score of 7 to 10 is considered high-risk. Where does your neighborhood fit in?

Danger Points

▲ Grass, weeds, shrubs +1
▲ Large shrubs, small trees +2
▲ Timber woodlands +3
▲ 1- to 10-degree slope +1
▲ 10- to 20-degree slope +2
▲ 20- to 40-degree slope +3
▲ 40-degree slope or more +4
▲ Less than 1 home per 10 acres +1
▲ 1 home per 5 to 10 acres +2
▲ 1 home per 0 to 5 acres +3
▲ Rough terrain +1
▲ History of fire +1
▲ Extreme fire weather +1

Safety Points

▲ Good water, −1
   roads, signs
▲ Strict local −1
   fire ordinances

3

▲▲▲▲▲▲▲▲▲▲▲▲▲▲ 3 ▲▲▲▲▲▲▲▲▲▲▲▲▲▲

The Unique Triangle:
Wind, Temperature,
Humidity

Toward the end of each California summer, the hills turn brown and the wildland trees and shrubs settle into their best drought-survival mode until relieved by the fickle rains of late fall. If water supplies are low, plants in home landscapes are equally dry, leaves desiccated, moisture content low, and many that could not stand the water denial have died. The hot desert winds rustle the foliage of eucalyptus, and strips of thick, peeling bark crackle as they are blown down in heaps around the base of each tree. During these dog days the heat hangs low upon the land, air so dry it feels like a sprinkling of talcum powder upon the skin. Evenings are balmy and warm, the beaches beckon, and the activity of early summer has exhausted itself into a quiet peace.

But lurking beneath this bucolic scene is the ever present threat of fires, and many rural residents refuse to utter the word in superstitious fear, while others knock on wood. Fire weather in California relies on three conditions: wind, high temperatures, and low humidity. Whether or not there is a fire also depends on the availability of fuel.

It is easy to see why most people grow nervous when fire season begins in California. Arsonists tend to grow more excited under these conditions, knowing their efforts have the greatest chance of becoming a serious wildfire. Everyone should stay tuned to their local news and fre-

▲▲▲▲▲▲▲▲▲▲▲▲▲▲▲▲▲▲▲▲▲▲▲▲▲▲▲▲▲▲▲▲▲▲▲

quently scan the skies for the plumes of smoke that mark the start of a "big one." This is when it is most important for everyone to be extra cautious about any activity that could possibly ignite a fire.

Some of our most devastating fires first appeared as this one does: a wispy plume of smoke on a far-off horizon. The direction the smoke is pointing is the path flames are likely to travel when pushed by summer winds.

Wind

The prevailing wind in California during most of the year is off the Pacific Ocean, where it gathers moisture before reaching the coast. But in late summer and autumn, the sun has heated the surface of the soil and the air above it so completely that a pressure difference occurs. As air moves from higher pressure zones to those of lower pressure, wind results. In Northern California these are the northwest winds which whip down through the Sacramento and San Joaquin valleys to consume what little moisture still lingers there and in the foothills.

These foothills, the Coast Range on the west and the Sierra Nevada on the east, are cloaked in chaparral. The winds eddy in their undulating topography, which ranges from gently rolling hills to heavily vegetated, nearly vertical slopes. With each day of wind, chaparral plants and the surrounding grasslands grow drier as moisture is literally drawn out of the leaves by the wind.

In the southern portion of the state, the notorious Santa Ana winds, heated by desert sands of the Mojave, blow westward to parch much of the coastline as well as inland communities from Santa Barbara to San Diego. They may begin and cease mysteriously, and often fires driven by these winds are literally unstoppable until the Santa Anas finally die down.

Other versions of these same winds can blow over higher elevations in our mountain ranges during late summer. This is made even more dangerous when they are associated with afternoon thunderheads that produce violent lightning storms, and in the worst cases, rain never follows. Lightning storms of just this sort have been the historic source of natural fires in our mountain forests.

Temperature

In almost every major fire the weather was hot and daily temperatures consistently high. Heat from a flame will travel much further in warmer conditions than in cooler temperatures. For example, a neighbor had safely burned a pile of old board fencing in his field during the winter months. He accumulated a second, nearly identical pile of the same material by the middle of summer. But when he burned it on a warm afternoon the heat became far more intense, radiating out over a much bigger circle around the burn pile. In fact, it became so hot the paint on his home blistered and he feared it would ignite before the burn pile could be extinguished. The single difference in these two fires was ambient air temperature.

FIRESCAPING TIP

Fire experts tell us a campfire in 40-degree air warms an area about *two* feet on all sides. That same fire in 90-degree summer temperatures warms an area *twenty* feet on all sides. Evaluate the size and influence of your burn pile accordingly.

Another factor relating to temperature is the state of plants, both native and introduced species. Evapotranspiration is a word used to describe evaporation of moisture from both the soil surface and the leaves of a plant. In high temperatures, especially over weeks or months at a time, the evapotranspiration rate increases and plants lose vital moisture. As soil moisture evaporates to deeper and deeper levels, the reservoir available to plants diminishes.

Plants that have evolved with a resistance to drought conditions have deep root systems which access soil moisture during these high-stress periods. But under prolonged heat they too will eventually consume all soil moisture and then must turn to other methods of survival such as dormancy or defoliation. Plants less adapted to drought will die.

Plants subjected to heat and lack of moisture first cease to grow because there is insufficient water to carry on photosynthesis. Desert cacti evolved a unique mechanism of lying dormant during the day, their surface pores tightly closed against moisture loss in the heat. After sunset their pores, or stomata, open in order to begin photosynthesis during the night using stored light energy. But most plants are not so rugged.

The next drought mechanism is for plants to wilt because they do not contain sufficient moisture to keep the "turgidity" or water pressure up to par within their vessels. After that, the plant will defoliate by dropping all its leaves to reduce the foliage demand for moisture. With-

▲▲▲

The Ten Most Common Sources of Wildfires

According to the 1992 Wildfire Activity Statistics prepared by the CDF, these are the *known causes* of fires that year. Not included are fires of undetermined origin, or of unusual sources that do not fall into any of these known categories.

Cause	Number of Fires
1. Equipment use	1637
Examples: heavy equipment, farm implements, power tools.	
2. Vehicles	1001
Examples: recreational vehicles, automobiles, trucks, 4x4s.	
3. Arson	736
4. Lightning	682
5. Debris burning	637
Examples: burn barrels, rubbish heaps, leaves, slash piles.	
6. Campfires	535
Examples: fires outside campgrounds, transients.	
7. Playing with fire	300
Examples: firecrackers, matches	
8. Electrical power	279
Examples: tree limb abrasion, outdoor extension cords	
9. Smoking	235
10. Railroad	28

▲▲

out leaves some plants die, but others become temporarily dormant, as many California native plants do until the fall rains support a new crop of leaves. When plants die or defoliate they add that much more dry, volatile fuel for fires.

Humidity

Humidity is a term that refers to the amount of suspended moisture in the air. Southern California beach towns are perpetually moist, not because of rainfall, but due to the proximity of a large body of water. Air moisture is supplied by surface evaporation of water vapor from the soil, water bodies, and through transpiration of plants. *Relative humidity* is gauged by determining how much moisture the air could hold if it were saturated. Rain is close to 100% saturation but in contrast many California fire-weather scenarios registered only 20% humidity. The daily humidity percentages are usually mentioned on radio or television weather broadcasts.

Water vapor remains in the air longer at lower temperatures. As heat increases it tends to dry up and humidity levels drop. This is how temperature and humidity are interrelated. Dead fuels are also influenced by this factor as they may contain a significant amount of moisture in humid conditions, but when humidity drops these tend to slowly dry out and become volatile fuels.

How Most California Wildfires Are Started

It is sad to say, but many of our worst fires are set intentionally by arsonists. These "torches" tend to become more active during fire weather or when other wildfires are already burning. In many cases the arsonist is fascinated by fire and remains on the scene to observe the flames. Sometimes he or she will actually help fire fighters. Police understand these and many other characteristics of arsonists and keep a sharp eye out on every fire scene for suspicious individuals.

Other fires are caused by negligence. This refers to people who know they are not supposed to burn rubbish, but do so anyway. Another example is "sneaking" a campfire after dark, when the smoke isn't visible, even when the forest rangers have made it clear fires are prohibited. Sometimes smokers will be careless while walking in high-fire-hazard wildlands, or toss a burning cigarette out the car window. All these fires can be avoided if people are cautious of fire danger and act accordingly.

There are many subtle ways a fire can start accidentally that most

FIRESCAPING TIP

It is ironic that many grass fires are started by conscientious home-owners trying to mow down dry grass around their homes in the late summer to reduce fire hazard. Fire experts say the time to mow is much earlier in the year, while grass is still green and less combustible. Fires ignite when tinder-dry clippings make contact with a hot engine or exhaust system. Sparks are also produced when the blade of a rotary mower hit rocks or dirt, a factor more insidious because it occurs out of sight, beneath the mower blade housing.

people aren't aware of. For example, an off-road vehicle such as a motorcycle can ignite dry grass with its hot engine or exhaust pipe. A wood cutter's hot chain saw set into dry leaves can easily begin a smouldering ground fire. Landscape tree limbs rubbing on power lines can work through the insulation and spark a fire.

A final source of fires, which occurs frequently in late summer in the Sierra Nevada, is lightning. The clouds rise from the eastern deserts into the forests, where there is plenty of fuel and difficult access. With luck a cloudburst will follow . . . but not always. We must live with these fires and accept them as part of the natural weather pattern of the mountains.

▲▲▲▲▲▲▲▲▲▲▲▲▲▲▲ 4 ▲▲▲▲▲▲▲▲▲▲▲▲▲▲▲

Water:
Your Essential Resource

Drive through any part of California from August through November and you'll probably find that all but the largest rivers have dried up for the season. Fire fighters are also faced with this shortage of their main tool for the ground crews. An important emergency source in most Sierra foothill regions is "ditch water," which runs through the fire season and is purchased by users along the ditch. The ditches are a remnant of the placer mining days of the Mother Lode. Ditches are often the only reliable source of water for fire fighting, and they also allow residents to keep their emergency reservoirs full. Unfortunately, the endangered species agencies have decided the smelt spawning in the Sacramento River Delta need the water more than these residents. There is now a serious attempt to eliminate these water districts, which leaves both residents and fire fighters high and dry. Meanwhile the smelt are having an orgy in the delta.

If fire fighters cannot obtain water to defend your home against an oncoming fire, there is little they can do. And in many cases there are insufficient numbers of crews to protect every home, so it is important to realize it may be up to *you* alone to protect your house.

Wildfires can be fast-moving, unpredictable and very dangerous. California law may not give you the option to remain and fight the fire if there has been an order to evacuate. Firestorms driven by high winds in large fuel volumes produce very high temperatures and dense smoke. Protecting your home to the bitter end can be deadly, so never remain behind if your escape route may be blocked by flame. Use com-

▲▲

mon sense and get out before your home is completely surrounded.

The availability of water is the single major factor in your ability to actively fight a wildfire. In rural areas with volunteer fire departments, a home water supply is also essential in putting out a house fire quickly, before major damage occurs. But the water supply is not your only concern. During these types of disasters, electrical lines often burn and cut off the power supply. Without electricity, you cannot operate a domestic well pump, or any other kind of pump for that matter. This shows how both water supply and the means to deliver it are equally important.

Efforts to put out the San Francisco blazes that followed the Loma Prieta earthquake were hindered by the loss of pressure and supply in the city water mains. Even if you are on a municipal system, the pressures needed by fire fighters at the hydrants will reduce the overall operating pressure, leaving very little for your efforts. Plus, if you are drawing water out of the system, it can work the other way to reduce pressure needed by fire fighters. This pressure loss can happen in any of our suburban communities and with increased crown fires occurring in cities, a home water supply independent of any municipal system is the only sure chance of fighting your own fire.

Design and installation of an emergency water supply and delivery system can be a complicated matter. There are many variables, such as the amount of water you have available, the distance it must travel to the point of delivery, and the flow demands. Flow demands relate to how much water is used over a certain amount of time. Eventually your supply will be exhausted and the more quickly you draw out the water, the shorter period of time you will be able to protect your home.

If you have not created a defensible space around your house, even the best emergency water system will have little, if any, impact on a full-scale wildfire. The information provided in this chapter is based on homesites that have not only created defensible space, but also maintain it correctly. **Consult with an expert when designing your system to be sure it is adequate and functions as intended.**

Emergency Water Supplies

The California Department of Forestry recommends that an emergency water reservoir for your home contain at least 2,500 gallons or more. Some building departments may require larger storage capacities, especially when very large homes or homesites are concerned. The more water you hold, the longer you are able to fight a fire. The reservoir should be located close to the house where you or the fire fighters and their equipment can gain access. A valve compatible with the equipment of local fire fighting agencies is helpful and may be stipulated by building codes.

There are many ways to create a reservoir that range in price and maintenance requirements. It is essential to evaluate purchase price, installation, maintenance, and longevity to be sure you are buying a reliable storage system. Water evaporates very quickly in hot, dry weather, and unless your water supply is fully contained and airtight, it will gradually dwindle away. It is essential to keep it consistently full at all times.

Domestic wells   Most homesites that are not supplied by a municipal water system rely exclusively on a domestic well. How much water the well produces is rated in gallons per minute, or GPM. In some foothill areas households survive on just 2 GPM, and require storage tanks because a mere water faucet draws at least 3 GPM. Other people are more fortunate, with wells producing anywhere from 10 to 100 GPM, and they can use a small pressure tank to meet their needs.

Heavily producing wells fed by water-filled underground caverns or rivers can make excellent emergency reservoirs. But most California wells are supplied by aquifers, which are deep gravel strata containing water. If a well fed by a slow-moving aquifer is pumped continually for a long period, it may exceed the speed of replenishment and dry up for a time until recharged. This is the problem with relying solely on a well for emergency water supply.

Swimming pools   The most versatile, but expensive large water reservoir for a homesite is a swimming pool. A standard size will contain more than enough water for most fire situations. Hot tubs and spas are smaller options, and there are many cases of their water saving a house. These present the greatest installation cost, but this is offset by the recreational use, which in Southern California can be for most of the year. There is also pool maintenance to consider, with chemicals and extensive mechanical systems. But a well-maintained pool is relatively free of debris, which can clog and disable your delivery system.

Aboveground vinyl-lined swimming pools such as the "Doughboy" also provide a considerable amount of water for fire fighting. These pools are not as long-lived as more traditional swimming pools because the liners tend to deteriorate over the years, and unless replaced may begin to leak. For homesites on sloping or rocky ground it may be difficult to set up one of these pools without extensive grading.

Ponds   Ponds are natural water bodies that must be filled periodically since they rely on the soil to retain water. Construction of a pond as fire reservoir should be well thought out before attempting to build. Rainfall is not sufficient in California to keep the pond full, and with a large surface area, moisture will evaporate very quickly. Be sure you have a reliable heavily producing spring or well to insure a consistent water level.

Construction of a functional and successful pond should be supervised by an engineer or representative from the USDA Soil Conservation Service. These experts are qualified to evaluate the location, design, and construction of a pond reliable enough for fire water. The soil must be analyzed for its water-holding capability because fissures and cracks in bedrock can allow water to percolate out of the pond rapidly. In this case only an expensive vinyl lining system will control the leaks. The walls must be graded properly for safety and to reduce the incidence of unwanted wetland vegetation that thrives in shallow water. Tules and cattails can eventually fill the entire pond, to restrict access to the water or displace it altogether. In some cases waterfowl will be drawn to the pond, which can create a mess along the banks, although for those who wish such a wetland ecosystem this may not be a liability.

Tanks   Where a swimming pool, productive well or a pond is not possible, a water tank is the next best choice. Tanks sold today are usually wood or plastic. Redwood tanks are more available in Northern California, particularly around the vineyard country where they were once used at wineries. Wood tanks resemble hot tubs and consist of a circular base fitted with upright boards for the walls held together with steel bands. Keep in mind a tank of any size can be difficult to set up and is best left to the experts.

A dry redwood tank has gaps between the slats of wood that make up the outside wall. When sufficiently wet the wood expands to close the gaps, thus sealing the tank. From this point on the tank must be kept full and at a consistent water level to prevent the gaps from reopening when the wood dries and shrinks. If there is no reliable water supply to keep the tank full at all times, it will begin to leak and waste what water there is as the wood contracts.

Finding a good redwood tank is no easy matter. Most of those that are sold as "used" are snatched up as soon as they become available, either by homeowners or tank resale and construction companies. Even an old tank is expensive, and the price of a newly manufactured one is exorbitant. However, there are no other aboveground tanks that blend into the landscape as beautifully. High cost, limited availability, complicated set-up, and the need for water level consistency are all reasons why redwood tanks are not more widely used.

With the advent of modern plastics there are now excellent heavy duty rigid tanks that make good alternatives to redwood. The plastic tanks are lightweight and simple to move around, although they do not break down into transportable units as with wood tanks. You will find there is a limit to sizes of plastic tanks which can be shipped by truck. Those that are cylindrical, say 6 feet in diameter, and 20 feet long will fit well on a tractor-trailer rig. A wider tank presents problems and may require a step-down trailer or a wide load permit, which will complicate shipping.

FIRESCAPING TIP

If you would like the option of taking a dip in your fire water tank, an open-topped model is available. The largest you can transport is 6 feet deep and 10 feet wide. This gives you a 10-foot diameter pool containing 3,500 gallons of water, a sufficient volume that won't heat up during the summer. It should be freestanding and have a double flange at the top. To improve water quality just fill and let it overflow for awhile. For the redwood tank "look," surround the outside with 6-foot-long cedar fence boards and secure them with two or three cables tightened by turnbuckles.

You can set up a plastic tank by simply leveling a spot on the ground and spreading a layer of gravel evenly upon the surface. Since plastic does not decompose like wood, it can be set directly upon the gravel bed and is instantly ready for use. Moving a plastic tank is simple; first empty the contents, then simply roll it across the ground. Most plastic tanks are geared for chemical containment, so they are long-lived, heavy duty, and surprisingly durable.

Plastic tanks are available in a wide variety of shapes and sizes to choose from. Some are fully enclosed upright cylinders with only a small opening at the top for cleaning and filling. Others resemble a gasoline station underground tank, which are large fully enclosed cylinders that lie horizontally upon the ground. Still others are cylinders with open tops like a wood tank or hot tub, available in a variety of sizes that are limited only by what can be safely transported upon the highway. A fire hose valve can be installed for you by the manufacturer.

Cisterns   A cistern is an underground water storage unit. Due to the excavation costs they tend to occur only on very old homesites or those in affluent neighborhoods where they are used for domestic potable water. The advantage to a cistern is that it is out of sight and not subjected to litter problems of open-water reservoirs. The water is insulated by the earth so it remains at an even cool temperature.

In the northern portions of the state, annual rainfall can reach 100 inches along the coast, which is an incredible amount of water. A lined underground cistern for *nonpotable* water can be fed all winter by rain gutters, then remain in reserve until fire season. These are enclosed systems with very low evaporation rates. Some people build their cisterns by burying a heavy plastic tank underground where it is out of site and low enough so that gravity will cause rain gutter downspouts to drain directly into the tank without pumps.

Pumping Fire Water

Even if you have the largest water supply in the Western World, when the electric lines burn and power is cut off, there is no means of pumping the water under pressure. One resident recently faced with an oncoming fire suddenly realized he could not access the 16,000 gallons in his underground cistern because the fire would burn his power lines long before it reached the house. Obtaining power to extract water from your reservoir and pressurize it sufficiently to make a difference is the other half of the emergency water supply equation.

The two basic means of supplying power to run your fire water pump are with a **gasoline electrical generator** or a **gasoline water pump**. The gasoline-powered generator is used to supply power to an electrically operated water pump that may already be in place. A gas water pump is a simpler, more direct means of pulling water out of a reservoir and pressurizing it for fire flows. These little pumps are inexpensive, portable, and easy to use so they may be kept indoors and out of the weather until needed.

If your water supply is a domestic well or underground cistern, it is accessed differently than other types of reservoirs. Water can be drawn by a submersible pump suspended by pipe down into the water. It is driven by electrical wires which extend from the power supply at the top of the well head, down the shaft to the pump. These wires then run from the well head to the house electrical breaker panel. But if there is a house fire, or fire close enough to damage the breaker or the lines extending to the pump, using a generator connected to the breaker will be useless. The best way to access well water is to attach the wiring at the well head directly to a gasoline-powered generator set beside it.

It pays to hire an electrician who can help you select a generator. He or she will take into consideration the demands of a fire water system and can also help you pick a generator with enough power to run your household during power failures of any kind. Many foothill residents were snowed in without power a few years ago and were forced to melt snow for water because they could not access their wells without electricity. The electrician will insure there are no mistakes which may burn out the pump or generator under prolonged use.

When in place, test the generator system a number of times to insure it starts easily and operates properly. Run the system for an hour or more because if you have not sized your wiring properly it will heat up to indicate the amperage draw is too high for your connection. The time to discover there is a problem with your system is *not* during a fire.

FIRESCAPING TIP

A good way to simplify a domestic well emergency fire system is to build a weather-tight well house or shed over the well and pressure tank if you have one. Design it so there is a safe place for the generator close enough to the well wiring to make quick connections safe and simple. This eliminates the need to bring the generator out to the well during a fire emergency.

Rodent damage can ruin parts of a pump, hose, or generator. Whenever possible protect or store these items away from chewing pests and check them frequently for any sign of damage. Keep in mind that a single wire chewed by a field mouse could cause the loss of your home.

To draw and push water out of other types of reservoirs such as tanks, ponds, and swimming pools, a gasoline-powered pump is the simplest method. These pumps vary in size and most are portable. It's a good idea to buy a pump that can be transported to the water source by *one* person, because there is no assurance a second person will be at home when the fire starts. If it is too heavy for one person to move, construct a weather- and rodent-proof house to store fire equipment close to the water source.

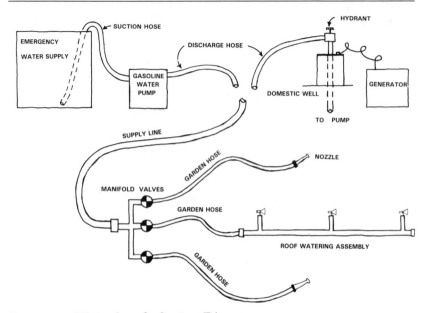

Emergency Water Supply System Diagram

This diagram shows the basic components of a water supply system using either a domestic well or another storage reservoir. This is schematic and does not take into consideration operating pressures or the final sizing of pipe or hose as this can vary considerably depending on the site.

There will be two places for hoses to be attached to the pump. One is the **suction port** where water is drawn out of the reservoir and through the pump mechanism. The water comes out the other side of the pump under pressure through the **discharge port**. You must have a hose of sufficient size to extend from the suction port to the deepest point in the reservoir to be able to use the entire water supply. The hose attached to the discharge port must be long enough to reach all parts of your house or any fire suppression systems you have devised. The pump should also be **self priming** so it becomes immediately useable. If your water source is not particularly clean there should be a filter or "suction strainer" at the end of your suction hose so that no debris will enter the system and clog nozzles or sprinklers.

Sizing the Pump

Water pumps vary in size, and there is certain criteria that is important to know in order to select a model sufficient for your needs. **Warning: To be sure you are buying the right sized pump for your emergency fire system, enlist the aid of a professional.** You will find assistance from a number of different government agencies depending upon where you live. Some counties or cities require a mandatory emergency fire system be installed at each home, and in this case they supply specific criteria for you to follow. The local municipal fire station may be able to send a professional to your home to help design a system. In rural areas the California Department of Forestry and Fire Protection, or the USDA Soil Conservation Service may be able to offer some help.

A registered civil engineer is probably the best resource, but he or she will require payment for consulting time and design services. The cost of a civil engineer is worthwhile when designing larger systems for rural homes, farms, or ranches. Factors such as friction loss must be calculated into a piping plan in order to prevent a loss of pressure over long runs of pipe. You will feel more confident with a pump selected by a professional who has factored in all the variables of your site.

FIRESCAPING TIP

You'll find there are two general classes of water pumps. Those that are labeled specifically as **fire pumps** are quite a bit more expensive than standard gasoline-powered water pumps. This is because these are used by professional fire fighters who demand certain qualities of their equipment. If you can afford one, these are the best and most reliable you can buy.

Important Definitions Relating to Sizing a Pump

Gallons per minute (GPM)   The amount of water passing a point in the line over a given time. This might also be labeled velocity of flow, or flow rate. Portable pumps used by fire-fighting agencies generally deliver 30 to 35 GPM through a 1½ inch diameter hose. Home systems may put out more than this, with 100 GPM ideal if the reservoir is large enough.

Pressure (PSI)   The energy or force of the water at a given point in the line. Expressed as pounds per square inch. Fire fighter's portable pumps deliver at about 75 to 90 PSI through a 1½ inch diameter hose.

Friction loss   The loss of pressure caused by water flowing in the system calculated according to each linear foot of pipe, its diameter, the number and type of fittings and the gallons per minute.

Feet of head, head pressure   This is a means of factoring in gravity demands on a pump. One foot of head equals .43 PSI. For example, if your water source is 100 feet *below* the roof of your house, in order to factor in gravity you will need at least 43 PSI added to standard operating pressures for water to reach the roof under adequate PSI. However, this must also be combined with friction loss as well. This illustrates how technical sizing of pumps, hoses, and piping layout can become on a large-scale system. It is suggested that an engineer or other qualified professional be enlisted to design or check your system components before you select a pump.

Horsepower   This is the way small gasoline engines are sized. The greater the horsepower, the more GPM the pump will push. This also relates to PSI, with larger engines needed for high pressure systems.

Electric start pump   Gasoline engines are usually fired up manually with a recoil start. More sophisticated models are available with push-button starting systems, which require a battery. Battery maintenance is critical to their reliability over the long term, so it may be wise to have a recoil start as backup.

Delivering Fire Water

Your water source will be the discharge port on your pump. The hose or its coupler must be the same diameter as the port, which usually ranges from 1 to 2 inches, but this does vary with each pump. Many pumps are rigged for a "lug coupler," which is a special brass fitting preferred for larger diameter connections and used by fire fighters. If your hose is smaller than the discharge port, you can attach reducing bushings to decrease the size.

Garden hose diameters range from ½ to ¾ inch, which is relatively small in fire fighting terms. They are also made of rubber and other materials that may melt easily in the event of a fire. For the most reliable system, it is recommended your main supply hose be a 1½-inch standard cotton-jacket fire hose designated for outdoor fires. Avoid hoses designed for use inside buildings such as those stored permanently in hallways of offices and hotels.

This large fire hose can extend from your reservoir to the house. Once there you can make a manifold which will split a single supply line into two or more smaller lines. This is why it is a good idea for the supply line to be as big as possible, because a smaller hose will not deliver very much water if split into multiple-delivery garden hoses. For example, if the main supply hose is ¾ inch and capable of delivering no more than 10 GPM, that would barely be enough for a sprinkler and a second hand-held hose. If you have more that one sprinkler set up on the roof, attaching this main hose to the sprinkler leaves you with no way to hand-spray hot spots.

It is best to use a main supply line of the same diameter as your discharge port, then construct a manifold that splits into three or four different lines. Attach a gate valve to each port on the manifold and buy a high-quality garden hose for every one. Also have variable brass nozzles on hand so that you can change from a long stream spray to mist with a simple adjustment, or even turn it off entirely without going back to the valve. This assembly allows you maximum control at both the gate valve and the brass nozzle.

It is important to discuss your manifold with a fire system consultant. Each time the supply line splits there will be a reduction in GPM as well as pressure. If there is no compensation for this at the pump or main supply line you may end up with an anemic flow. **The more water you demand of the system, the faster your reservoir will be depleted.**

FIRESCAPING TIP

There are more sophisticated home wildfire systems available that rely on fire-retardant, nontoxic chemical foam products. These are permanent roof systems that may be activated automatically to apply a layer of fire-retardant foam over the roof and exterior walls of your home. The foam remains effective only as long as it lingers intact, which is a limited period. These systems are effective, but very expensive, with installations ranging from $6,000 to $9,000 per home. Some smaller companies are developing a portable foam system which many feel shows great promise but may not be widely available or proven. To find out about contractors carrying these systems and related products contact your nearest fire station or fire fighting agency.

Roof Watering System

During a fire where embers are falling like rain, you can't be everywhere at once. It may surprise you how much area there is to cover on the average roof. The best way to keep it consistently moist is to use sprinklers. If you were to set up individual sprinklers you'd need a separate hose for each one. The best way to resolve this is to make your own miniature sprinkler system that is designed to fit the contours of your roof.

The easiest way to cover a roof is to supply water at the ridgeline so it may run down both sides evenly. Spray sprinklers such as impact heads will lose a lot of water to evaporation as it flies through the air, particularly in the heat of a oncoming fire. One alternative is the soaker hose, which has tiny holes pricked all along its length. Lay one of these on each side of the ridgeline and there will be less evaporation and better saturation of the entire roof surface. Other products such as leaky pipe and some new alternatives are worth investigating, but they must be able to hold up over the years in storage without breaking down.

This is not to say spray heads are taboo. A basic ½- or ¾-inch PVC plastic pipe with two or three risers topped with sprinklers can be easily made at home. Add a sprinkler hose coupler to one end and cap off the other. This gives you plenty of coverage if placed along the ridgeline. If you have a manifold on your supply line you can set up these sprinklers and then be free to travel around the house to put out embers and spot fires with another hose line.

▲▲▲▲▲▲▲▲▲▲▲▲▲▲▲▲   ▲▲▲▲▲▲▲▲▲▲▲▲▲▲▲▲

Concepts Used in Fire-Resistant Landscapes: Managing Native Vegetation

The wildland-urban interface is a term coined to describe the increasing exposure of homesites to the threat of wildland fires. At a 1988 symposium of fire fighting agencies this interface was detailed as occurring in three basic situations. Think carefully about each one before purchasing a house. Pause and consider the surroundings of your current house and then decide if there is anything you can do to reduce the risk to your own property, or that of the entire community.

The **classic interface** involves homes and subdivisions growing around the edges of cities where younger families prefer to live. Most commute to work. These areas may appear more secure from fire threat than they actually are. Paved streets and fire hydrants, along with extensive landscaping all project a suburban character, yet as the crow flies these homes may be surprisingly close to high-fuel-volume wildland.

The **mixed interface** consists of more scattered developments, smaller subdivisions with larger parcel sizes. Ranchettes, vacation homes, and single isolated homesites can be completely surrounded by extensive wildland. Those who choose this lifestyle are interested in preservation of the natural environment, wildlife, and native vegetation. Although foresters and land managers suggest we must step in and assist in maintaining healthy wildlands, these homeowners are hesitant to disturb "pristine" countryside. Rural planning departments also

▲▲▲▲▲▲▲▲▲▲▲▲▲▲▲▲▲▲▲▲▲▲▲▲▲▲▲▲▲▲▲▲▲▲▲▲▲▲

tend to follow this path. Many county ordinances strictly control or outlaw the removal of trees and other vegetation either for aesthetic reasons or when wildlife agencies deem it habitat. The truth is that the countryside lost its virginity with the first Spanish settlers and the seeds brought to the New World in the wool of their sheep.

In the mixed interface, tremendous fuel volumes can accumulate due to restrictions as mentioned above, and from other side effects of urbanization. For example, vegetation that is disturbed, but not removed, becomes less healthy and subjected to disease and pests such as the pine bark beetle or oak root fungus. Our native oaks tolerate *no* disturbance to their root zone and will promptly die if preserved on site while surroundings have been altered. Paving, grading, livestock grazing, introduction of irrigation water, and changes to groundwater levels all contribute to the decline of plant communities in these areas. One expert stated that near Lake Arrowhead at least 50 percent of the pines were damaged by just this sort of "people pressure." The organization of Neighbors for Defensible Space live within this scenario and their fire danger grew to such great proportions they took active measures to insure their homes would not perish. But similar quasi-rural neighborhoods throughout California are still living in ignorant bliss amidst an overgrown, volatile countryside.

The **occluded interface** is more subtle than these first two. It deals with sometimes highly developed urban areas that contain unmanaged open or uncultivated spaces left to build fuel volumes. In 1985 three homeowners died when an eight-acre fire within the Los Angeles metropolitan area swept up a steep slope and overran their homes. A more current example is the Berkeley Hills fire, in an area hardly considered rural or even suburban.

Many unmanaged open spaces in urban areas are a result of undevelopable land such as overly steep slopes. Cut-and-fill subdivisions may have 2:1 slopes between building pads which are difficult to negotiate and manage. Throughout California these areas are threaded throughout subdivisions, with some irrigated and landscaped. They tend to be vegetated with drought-tolerant but volatile acacia and eucalyptus species as well as mounding woody groundcovers for erosion control and can accumulate tremendous amounts of fuel if not regularly pruned. In some cases these areas are extensive and considered an "open space" amenity to be left naturally vegetated or landscaped to separate clusters of high-density housing. In all of these cases there is a single common denominator; accumulations of vegetation and fuel loads. It is up to the homeowner to manage the areas around his or her immediate homesite as much as possible because leaving it to association maintenance services, the city, or simply ignoring it all together can be deadly.

In recent years developers planning new housing in areas deemed wetlands by the California Department of Fish and Game have been forced to compensate for the loss of habitat by setting aside areas within their projects for reestablishment of new wetlands. Due to our dry climate, preserved wetlands or newly created wetland habitat areas may be green and moist for only a few months of the year. Unlike a maintained and irrigated public park, these habitat spaces become choked with orchard grasses, tules, blackberry vines, and wild grapevines, the ideal cover for wild animals and birds. But during fire season in the late summer and fall this dense vegetation grows dangerously dry, and fires are likely to become a problem, particularly if the urban crown fires occur and flames travel quickly throughout the subdivisions via rooftops and landscape tree canopies.

Unless some sort of management program is enacted, these high concentrations of fuel will accumulate, making wetland habitats the source of dangerous occluded interface fires which threaten adjacent homes. Perhaps a better solution would be to ask developers to purchase land away from developments to increase the sizes of existing wildlife refuges. There animals and birds could find safe habitat in a more holistic environment instead of in tiny pockets in the middle of high-density housing.

Everyone Is at Risk

The mistake most Californians make is thinking that because there is a fire hydrant down the street it automatically protects them from wildfire. As illustrated in occluded interface scenarios, this is not always the case. Although a small city lot is easier to keep fire safe, there are still many things you must do to reduce the possibility of embers generated in open-space fires igniting the home. Homes in Berkeley Hills and Laguna Beach are perfect examples of this risk. Most were located on tiny lots, yet they burned out of control with the same speed and intensity of a wildland forest fire.

It is actually the classic and mixed interfaces that are at greatest risk because of the surrounding wildlands and spotty leapfrog development patterns. Concepts for protecting these homes through vegetation management begin with understanding the definition of **defensible space**. This is simply a band of managed vegetation around a home that slows the movement of fire by denying fuel and provides a space for fire fighters to take a stand to protect the house. When entire communities are threatened there may not be enough fire fighters or equipment to protect every home. **Fire fighters are more likely to take a stand at homes with defensible space than at those which cannot be separated from the surrounding vegetation.** Naturally you will want your house to be one of these chosen few.

Creating a Defensible Space

The overall size of your defensible space is based on the topography and limits of your property. The steeper the slope of your homesite, the larger an area is needed for a defensible space. This is because fire travels much more quickly uphill than it does on level ground and it is difficult for fire fighters to access steeper sites. To compensate, a larger area must be controlled.

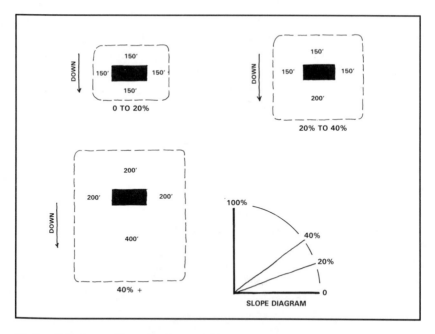

Defensible Space Boundaries and Slope Diagram

The outside limit of defensible space should be measured from the nearest building wall and extends outward from 150 feet to 400 feet. The required distance increases as slopes become steeper. The down-hill dimension is always larger because this is where fire and heat raging up the slope can be slowed by lack of fuel and hopefully stopped before it reaches the house. The slope diagram shows how steep slopes are that apply to each example.

The minimum area for homes on less than a **20 percent** slope should extend outward 100 feet on every side. If the house is on a **20 to 40 percent** slope, which is fairly steep, you will need to extend 150 feet uphill, 150 feet on each side, and 200 feet downhill. For slopes **over 40 percent**, manage 200 feet uphill, 200 feet on each side and 400 feet downhill. It's best to check with local government, because some communities may be more restrictive.

FIRESCAPING TIP

If your lot size is small, creation of a defensible space may require management of vegetation on the adjacent property as well as your own. It is illegal to alter or remove vegetation on property you do not own, and if it is done on government lands there may be serious penalties. If you must control vegetation on adjacent property, obtain permission from the owner (preferably written) *before* starting work. If it is government land contact the closest CDF station or local fire agency to find out which agency has jurisdiction and what laws govern its management.

Literature on basic homesite clearing is available statewide, but the defensible space concept takes this idea further to create a manageable area that is larger and more attractive. Simply clearing the ground of vegetation does reduce fire hazard, but it also creates an environment for soil erosion. Firescaping the defensible space is the best way to eliminate the erosion potential and improve the visual quality of a homesite.

The defensible space of each homesite is divided into three distinct conditions or bands radiating outward from around the house. Firescaping deals with the management of existing vegetation within the bands, and the addition of ornamental plants with fire-resistant qualities or naturally low fuel volumes. The first step is to define the limits of each band at your homesite and then take care of existing vegetation accordingly.

Zone 1 is the first 5 to 10 feet around the outside walls of the house. Combustible materials in this area are close enough to bring the fire in contact with the building wall, deck, or porch. Planting and landscaping is best limited to very succulent groundcovers, gravel mulches, walkways, and green lawns. If you have limited water supply for irrigation, let it be concentrated here.

Zone 2 begins at the perimeter of zone 1 and extends outward about 30 feet. Plants in this zone may be a combination of both native and introduced species. Trees must be widely spaced to prevent crown fires. Shrubs should be low-growing and preferably with high moisture content. Groundcovers, lawn, or mowed irrigated pasture are also acceptable. Due to the size and open nature of this area, fire fighters are likely to take a stand here to defend your home.

Zone 3 includes natural vegetation that has been modified to reduce available fuel volumes. The width of this band extends to the limit of the defensible space required according to topography as described above. The goal is to thin out overcrowded native plants, eliminate ladder fuels, and remove any dead plants or portions of plants that may spread fire. Fire resistant plants can be used here to improve visual quality.

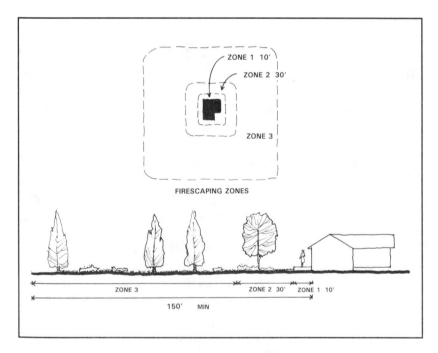

Plan and Section Views of Fire Band Locations

Fire zones 1 and 2 always remain the same as they radiate first 10 feet then another 30 feet from the walls of the house. If the house has an irregular shape, use the outermost points to begin measuring. The ultimate size of zone 3 can range from 110 feet to as much as 260 feet depending on topography.

▲▲

Firescaping Plant Spacing Guidelines at a Glance

The following guidelines are designed to break the continuity of fuel masses, which will interrupt the spread of flame from one plant to the other, or vertical movements via ladder fuels.

Trees   Minimum from the edge of one tree canopy to the edge of the next one according to topography:

0 to 20% slope = 10 feet
20 to 40% slope = 20 feet
40% and over = 30 feet.

Remove all limbs to 15 feet above the ground, but no more than one third of the tree's total height.

Shrubs   Zones 2 and 3—spacing is at least five times the height of the shrub.

Warning: If you must remove sizeable trees beware if their trunks are over 6 inches in diameter at your chest height. These are more safely removed by professionals. Trees are extremely heavy and sometimes unpredictable when they fall, often splintering and breaking into pieces. Consider power and telephone lines, structures, fencing, degree of slope, and wind before attempting to fell a tree. For assistance, consult a professional forester for advice, and/or a reputable tree service to do the job safely.

▲▲

Removal and Reduction: Modifying Native Vegetation

Not every homesite threatened by fire will have native vegetation. In many cases the landscape is barren as a result of large-scale grading and new construction. Older, established homesites may be well vegetated with introduced species that have naturalized in our climate or are growing under irrigation. Trees, shrubs, and vines growing without supplemental watering behave very much like our volatile native plant communities and should be treated as such. Species that are highly volatile and should be removed altogether include acacia, eucalyptus, pampas grass, and hopseed bush, to name just a few. See the extended listing in chapter 6. The first goal in creating a defensible space is to selectively remove plants, then prune to reduce fuel volumes of those that remain.

Creating a firescape around your home may involve either "re-modeling" an existing landscape, or the design of an entire landscape from scratch. In either case the same concepts will apply. Some people who have just moved to a rural area have a love affair with native vegetation and the suggestion of removing trees and shrubs is viewed as a mortal sin. But it is important to realize California's chaparral and forest areas are unnaturally overgrown and suffering from keen competition for what little soil nutrients and moisture is available. Thinning is actually beneficial and results in much healthier ecosystems.

A review of important terms:

Surface fire   Consumes fuels close to the ground. These can be dead material such as fallen leaves, twigs, and branches, or living fuels such as shrubs, grasses, and tree branches close to the ground.

Crown fire   Travels through tree tops consuming live fuel.

Ladder fuels   Flammable materials occurring between surface fires and crown fires which act as a ladder to either raise a surface fire to tree crowns, or bring a crown fire down to the surface.

Tree or shrub canopy   The overall diameter of the foliage head from edge to edge.

Managing the Oak Woodland

Our California grasslands cover most of the coastal areas, valleys, and lower tips of the foothills. It was once comprised of native grass species but today, many other grasses, sedges, and weeds of all sorts have naturalized. There are shrubs gradually moving into grasslands and many sites may contain large colonies of sage and ceanothus, which increase fire intensity and act as ladder fuels. The primary threat in this ecosystem is the spread of grass fires and their ability to move quickly into areas with homes or outbuildings.

The best way to control naturally occurring, unirrigated grasses is by mowing early in the season. If left to go to seed, some species can reach three feet tall with thick, stringy stems. If mowed when long there will be large amounts of chaff left, either standing or in flammable layers, which should be raked up and removed. Mowing dry grass with power tools is also a serious fire hazard in itself and is not recommended. If grass is mowed while still green and short, then left to grow a few more inches and mowed once again, the smaller clippings tend to decompose with early season moisture.

The best way to stop a grass fire is to deny it fuel. Because grass fires

The parklike setting of California's rolling grasslands studded by oak woodlands. Fire moves quickly through this ecosystem but tends to burn at lower temperatures.

tend to be of low intensity but fast moving, they can be suppressed more easily by firebreaks. A gravel road or pathway around the house in zone 2 should be sufficient if there are no trees or ladder fuels. It is recommended these barriers be at least five times the height of the uncut grass.

To create defensible space in zones 2 and 3, first remove all dead fuels. This includes lumber piles, unused sheds, standing dead trees, down dead trees, dead shrubs, branches, and accumulations of leaves

A fence line and windrow of trees were sufficient for fire fighters to stop this grassfire. The gravel road would also have served as a fire break before the flames reached this ranch.

The gravel driveway of this site is directed around the front of the lot with attractive planting areas in the center. This is an effective means of separating natural grasslands from the landscape and house.

or needles. If there are living trees and shrubs interspersed with the grasses they can act as ladder fuels. Trees should have both live and dead limbs removed from 10 to 15 feet above the ground. Because slopes in this plant community tend to be gradual, each tree should be spaced so there is at least 10 feet between its canopy edge and that of the next tree to check crown fires. Shrubs should be kept trimmed and thinned to appropriate spacing. Cut away any dead or dying material around the bases.

Managing Chaparral

Chaparral shrubs and trees burn very hot and produce tall flames. From them come burning embers which can ignite homes and landscape plants. Chaparral tends to grow in an unbroken sea of dense vegetation that creates a fuel-rich avenue through which the fire can travel unchecked. The overall goal in managing these plants is to thin and remove them so the continuity is broken up enough to slow the fire and provide an opportunity for fire fighters to get around freely.

For many homesites attacking the manzanita thickets may seem an overwhelming task. Some prefer to use heavy equipment to punch through large areas first before doing the hand work, particularly if extensive colonies of poison oak are present. This is understandable as long as there are no downhill water bodies vulnerable to siltation from disturbed soil runoff, and if erosion-control seed mixes are sown the

▲▲

Disposing of Slash

Whether you are working in the woodland, chaparral, or forest ecosystem, there may be considerable amounts of slash consisting of removed trees, shrubs, leaves, needles, twigs, and branches. Where dozer work has been carried out, there may be huge mounds of stuff. If you can't deal with it right away, it's better to separate the material into widely spaced smaller piles than one or two massive ones. Instruct your dozer operator to do this *before* he begins working on the site so you won't have to divide the piles afterwards. There are four main ways to dispose of the slash:

1. Use a chipper/shredder and grind the smaller material into useful mulch.
2. Salvage any and all firewood. Although this can be tedious in chaparral areas, this takes advantage of a free resource.
3. Haul it to a landfill. This can be difficult and expensive for large jobs, but if work is done in smaller increments it is manageable.
4. Burn the piles. In rural areas burning is done during the winter, and requires the landowner obtain a permit from the CDF or local fire agency. The permit may only be used during certain periods. Some people cover their slash piles with tarps or plastic sheeting to keep them dry in rainy weather until ready to burn. More on agricultural burning in chapter 10.

▲▲

same year. The first step is to begin thinning the trees and shrubs to appropriate spacing. Remove all debris created by hand work and the heavy equipment.

Begin chaparral management by removing all native shrubs in zone 1. In zone 2 retain only low-fuel-volume plants less than 18 inches tall and space those that are to remain as indicated on page 61. You can also group one to three shrubs together into small "islands" and treat them as a single plant. Cut away ladder fuels in all trees and be sure they are properly spaced. Zone 3 shrubs and trees should be spaced as indicated above. Keep these shrubs trimmed and free of any dead combustible material. If dozers have done some of the clearing, there may be a few latent deaths of plants unable to tolerate the soil disturbance. Remove these plants as they appear.

Managing Forest

Since the advent of fire suppression, our forests have become unusually thick with saplings that fill every small space where there is sufficient sunlight. The litter of fallen branches, cones, and thick layers of needles has accumulated for many decades. Although much of this will eventually decompose, it is being deposited at a much faster rate than decomposition. The pines have ladders of dead branches radiating out from their trunks waiting to transfer flames from a ground fire into the crowns. Dense fields of mountain shrubs completely blanket the ground in some areas. The key with this kind of environment is to thin the plants, clean up the ground, and discourage any new seedlings or stump sprouts.

Because many California residences are located in national forests or similar protected areas, cutting trees over a certain diameter may be prohibited. **Check with your local government to see if tree-cutting permits are required before thinning the forest on your site.** Remove all dead trees whether standing, leaning, or down. On large sites leave

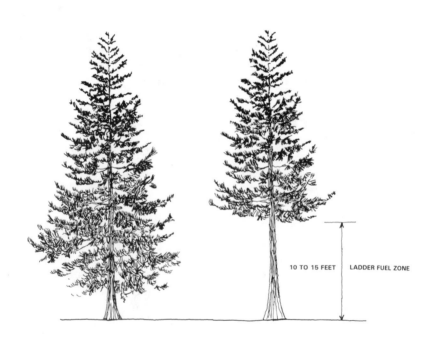

10 TO 15 FEET   LADDER FUEL ZONE

Trimming Ladder Fuels From Trees

The lower branches of trees become the ideal ladder fuel to transport flames from ground level to tree canopies. Ponderosa pines and similar species have a tendency for the lower branches to die, but remain attached to the trunk. Tinder-dry, these make excellent kindling and are highly flammable. All dead and living lower branches of every tree should be removed to at least ten to fifteen feet above the ground. If there is a shrub located within the dripline of the tree, the lowest branch should be at least three times as high as the shrub.

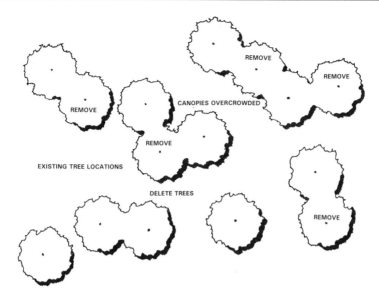

Example of An Existing Tree Layout

Many of these trees have canopies that touch or overlap, which creates an unbroken aerial fuel mass. Some trees will have to be removed so that each one stands alone, and is spaced the appropriate distance from the next tree, and that span depends on slope.

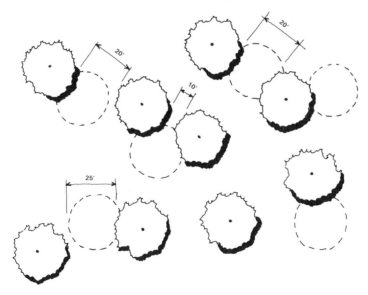

Tree Removal Diagram

The first trees to be removed should always be those weakened by damage or disease. Of those that remain, remove trees that would render the spacings at the appropriate distances. You don't want to take out any more trees than is necessary because they contribute to soil stabilization, shading, and aesthetic beauty of the landscape.

one or two dead trees per acre for habitat, but remove all the side branches. Thin remaining trees to appropriate spacing and remove ladder fuels to 15 feet above the ground. Remove all dead fuels. Thin shrubs to proper spacing to break continuity if possible and keep to 18 inches tall.

FIRESCAPING TIPS

1. Plants have a limited lifespan and a healthy ecosystem is always in a state of transition. New seedlings sprout to someday make up for the loss of their parent tree, much like people have children to carry on their families. To keep your property healthy and diverse, it's a good idea to select a few of the healthiest baby trees and preserve them within the fire band zones for the future.

2. The thinning of trees to separate the canopies within a firescape should be begun by removing those individuals which may be unhealthy or display undesirable growth characteristics. Trees with problems could prove short-lived so healthy ones must be given top priority. Closely inspect each one of your trees for the following imperfections:

▲ Abundance of mistletoe.

▲ Bark—cankers, blistering, discoloration, splitting, unusual peeling, signs of insect tunnels, large ant colonies, oak balls.

▲ Damage—girdling, unusual sap accumulations, torn bark, cracking at branch axils, stunted growth, wildlife damage.

▲ Foliage—premature leaf drop, tip dieback, discoloration, mildew, black residue.

▲ Form—unusual twisting of trunk, low weak forking, broken top of conifers, leaning, abundant surface rooting.

6

Ornamental Plants and Irrigation for Firescaping

S ome of the worst of California's suburban fires occurred on hillside subdivisions such as those in Berkeley Hills, Bel Air, and Laguna Beach. One factor that influences landscapes in areas such as these is erosion control on both cut slopes and those composed of fill. Drought-tolerant soil-stabilizing plants are widely used with combinations of trees and shrubs. In older neighborhoods these plants will be fully mature with accumulations of litter and dead wood because maintenance can be difficult on steep slopes and is often ignored. When these dense, overgrown slope plantings are desiccated by drought they become highly volatile.

Erosion was a serious concern of Neighbors for Defensible Space when designing their program because a large number of homesites in Incline Village were on ground sloping down to the edge of Lake Tahoe. Their fear was that bare or disturbed soil produced by fuel management could have disastrous effects on water quality in Lake Tahoe. The increased runoff and siltation would have to be eliminated or at least mitigated if their program was to be accepted by various government agencies concerned about wildlife habitat and water quality.

Although most of us need not be concerned about dirtying Lake Tahoe, everyone must be aware of potential soil erosion. If left bare and thus nonflammable, slope integrity could be compromised, and devastating mud slides are all too common in California, especially when protective vegetation has been removed by mass grading or fires. Gradual erosion can pit and furrow the slopes or weaken fill materials beneath the surface, where water seeks weaknesses in soil compaction. Therefore, it is a given that any firescape plan on sloping ground must be concerned with erosion control.

The replacement of vegetation or installation of new plants in a firescape occurs mainly in fire bands 1 and 2, those closest to the house. If there is no existing vegetation in zone 3, then planting must also occur there. Before going into the details of plants suitable for these areas, there are important criteria to be considered.

Irrigation: The Great Qualifier

The single factor that governs volatility of plant material is moisture content. A naturally fire-retardant plant such as iceplant will dry up and become surface fuel if denied enough water for the leaves to retain their succulent nature. The big problem facing Californians, particularly those who own large homesites, is the availability of water to irrigate their firescape plantings. If mandatory water rationing is imposed on those dependent upon municipal water systems, the entire firescape may be left to die without any irrigation at all. Future droughts are inevitable, so the best we can hope for is to design the firescape so it uses all the water at our disposal in the most efficient manner possible.

Over the last two decades there has been a revolution in the world of irrigation. The traditional spray system of high-volume misting heads is falling by the wayside. These heads are not efficient users of water for the following reasons:

1. A portion of the water evaporates into the air from the mist long before it reaches plants and soil.
2. Wind can blow the spray out of planting areas to reduce coverage and even leave some spots completely dry.
3. Blanket coverage waters areas of soil that do not support plant life except weeds.
4. Heads often deliver water at rates greater than the soil can absorb, which results in wasteful runoff.

Plants for firescaping and erosion control tend to be low-growing groundcover species. These can cover large areas of ground in two ways. First are **creeping shrubs**, which consist of single plants that grow into very large diameters. Only a few plants may be required to cover an area, although they may take years to reach mature size. Planting them more densely will reduce this time period, but it is still slow. Examples are mat-like manzanita or dwarf coyotebush.

The second group are **spreading plants**, which are more like typical groundcovers with many individuals planted at spacings from 6 to 12 inches apart. These rooted cuttings may strike roots as they grow and eventually fill in gaps, but the rate varies with each species. Examples are hypericum or ajuga. The reason it is important to distinguish these two types of groundcovers is that each are watered in a different way.

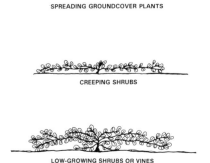

SPREADING GROUNDCOVER PLANTS

CREEPING SHRUBS

LOW-GROWING SHRUBS OR VINES

Variations In Groundcover Plants

Plants with low-growing profiles that spread out to cover large areas of soil can be herbaceous spreaders, creeping shrubs, and vines which become groundcovers when denied a vertical support. Each is planted, tended, and irrigated in a different way.

The newest techniques in efficient irrigation are drip systems and microspray systems. They both deliver water at such a slow rate their emitters are gauged at gallons per hour (GPH), rather than the gallons per minute (GPM) of traditional spray systems. Drip systems operate under low pressure with the flexible piping either underground, buried beneath mulch or left above ground. Emitters are located at individual plants to wet their root zone and nowhere else. Drip systems tend to concentrate water so it saturates more deeply into the soil and encourages adventurous rooting. The more extensive the root zone, the better able the plant to resist drought.

Microspray heads are just as easy to install because they require the same piping as a drip system, but use a different type of emitter. Each microspray head actually sprays in a circular pattern with a radius of about 8 to 10 inches. The assembly includes a pencil-like spike that is forced by hand into the ground, but can be pulled up and moved around easily because of the flexible supply tubing. The head sits only a few inches above the soil surface so there is less exposure to wind, and a shorter distance to spray, which reduces evaporation. You can easily add or subtract heads as you please because the water demands of each one is minimal.

Each creeping shrub in your firescape may be watered by a drip emitter or microspray head. But for spreading plants with sometimes dozens of individuals, it is not always feasible to supply that many drip emitters in such a concentrated area. Microspray heads might serve more than one spreading plant, but over time the entire area may require coverage for the mature stand to remain sufficiently moist and thus fire resistant. This many heads can also make it very difficult and inconvenient to mow herbaceous groundcovers. Keep this in mind when designing your planting plan because without comprehensive irrigation the plants may die or lose their fire-resistant qualities.

If you are faced with a serious water shortage, there is no choice but to design your firescape to work with drip and microspray systems. For best results the bulk of the area should be planted in large-diameter creeping shrubs and a few widely spaced trees which all can be easily watered by an emitter drip system. To inject more color and interest, smaller zones of spreading plants can be spotted in. Size these zones so each requires from three to five microspray heads.

Last Resort or Water Harvesting
When mandatory water rationing barely allows enough water for bathing and dishes, even a drip system may become too demanding. Under these conditions, which are usually serious droughts, the fire hazard reaches peak levels. To let the firescape wither and die at this time would leave you extremely vulnerable. No matter how much effort is required, do everything you can to preserve the moisture content of these plants.

If you lived on the Washington state coastline, it may rain periodically during the summer, but this is a rare occurrence here in California during fire season. The idea of storing accumulated rain water from downspouts might be a good idea, but Southern California does not receive enough rainfall each winter to make it worthwhile. Perhaps further north the possibility increases, but you will need an enclosed storage tank not subject to high levels of evaporation. An underground cistern is ideal, but expensive. Fifty-gallon drums are a possibility, but very heavy when full if they must be moved closer to where water is needed.

Imagine how much water is required to fill your washing machine for a sizeable load. This can range from 15 to 20 gallons, and during a normal cycle it will drain after the wash phase, fill a second time, then drain out again. That is two full drums of water wasted into the sewer. This is why **gray water** utilization, although a nasty term for illegal activity according to most city codes, can mean the difference between a defensible space and a dry, dead volatile one. The reason it is frowned upon is that harmful bacteria can accumulate if gray water is stored for any length of time. The key is to use it immediately rather than store for later use.

Laundry water is a good source of emergency firescape water because it does not contain grease and food as does dishwater. Laundry is done frequently throughout every season, so there is a constant fresh supply without storage problems. If detergents used are free of dyes and perfumes, the water will contain some nutrients beneficial to plants. However, if water is concentrated and these minerals build up to toxic levels, plants may suffer. When the rinse water is combined with the wash water, the residual detergent is further diluted.

If you remove the drain hose from your sewer standing drain pipe and rig it to drain instead into a barrel outside, you can then ladle out water into buckets to water your plants. You may also be able to devise a siphon system to eliminate the labor of hoisting buckets of water. Firescapes using trees and spreading shrubs are easier to water by this method because you will have fewer individual plants to water, and you can fashion a soil basin around each one to hold the water until it soaks in.

Another source is bathwater. It can be left in the tub and carried outdoors by the bucketful to pour around plants. Sure, you say, "When am I going to find the time to carry all these buckets of water outside?" The reply is that you are guaranteed to be far busier arranging to rebuild your house after it is burned to the ground, than you would be emergency bucket feeding your firescape.

Plants for Firescape Bands

There are no fireproof plants—they will all burn in an intense fire. But we can select plant species that have an ability to resist fire through unusually high moisture content and those that provide the least amount of fuel to an approaching wildfire. How we arrange and space these plants is also important to interrupting fuel availability. The following are definitions of terms used in this book, which are important in order to avoid misunderstandings.

Fire resistant This is a *relative* term used to describe plants that are "more resistant" or "less resistant" than other plants. These more resistant plants are made so by higher amounts of moisture within twigs and foliage. Under a low or moderately intense fire, they may be slower to burn, but a really strong fire will char them in a minute. A fire-resistant plant can lose this quality altogether if not properly maintained and irrigated.

Low fuel volume   This refers to the amount of fuel an individual plant contributes to an oncoming fire. It relates primarily to size and height. For example, a well-maintained ground-hugging species of manzanita offers very little if any fuel above 12 inches high for a fire to burn, but an upright inland manzanita species consists of three to five times as much burnable fuel per plant. A naturally low-growing plant allowed to build up dead wood and a mounding habit due to neglect becomes a fire hazard and no longer has a low fuel volume.

Notice how a plant labeled as fire resistant or having a low fuel volume can actually lose these characteristics unless properly maintained. This single concept is pivotal in the long term effectiveness of a firescape band system.

Group I   Greatest Fire Resistance

Studies have shown that plant species that retain high levels of moisture in their leaves and stems are the most fire resistant. In every case, these are always succulents. There are some misunderstandings about the fact that succulents have evolved to survive periods of drought by storing moisture in their leaves. This is true, but during these dry times the

This green carpet is one of the manzanita species listed in the Group II plant list. It is nearly as ground hugging as lawn and is a very attractive drought-tolerant California native landscape plan. It's easy to see how little fuel the plan would offer to an oncoming fire.

Another manzanita species native to the chaparral belt of the Sierra. It is an extremely volatile plant and grows in thickets with digger pine and oak as shown in the background. This manzanita is undesirable in firescapes unless treated like a tree and spaced a considerable distance from other fuels.

plants will pucker, wither, and a large portion may die off, depending on the length and severity of the drought. If the succulent is to grow, thicken, and retain its fire resistant qualities, it must be watered frequently. At the Huntington Botanical Garden in Southern California, the succulents are watered almost every week during the summer months.

The succulents listed as having sufficient fire resistant qualities for fire bands are primarily iceplants. Like palms, these plants have been long maligned in the southland because of their great popularity during the 1960s. It seems as though plants that become trendy can just as quickly be considered tacky and in poor taste. At the turn of the century cacti and succulent gardens were everywhere in California, their unique shapes and intensely colorful flowers considered new and different by immigrants from cold eastern states. Resurrected, iceplants present one of our most promising firescaping groups as water supplies dwindle, because fire-resistant landscape plants that offer such brilliant color are few and far between.

The list of succulent plants accepted by most Southern California cities and counties as the most fire resistant are comprised of plants with different growth characteristics. Do not assume they are all groundcovers. Some, such as the agaves and aloes, are slow-growing, small plants with tall bloom spikes. Others simply develop into neat, compact plants. Of course those which mound or spread will cover the greatest area of bare ground. Iceplant is a generic term given to a vast family of groundcovers comprised of many different genera. Flower color varies as well as leaf size and shape. The chief enemies of all succulents are intense cold, shade, soggy soil, and an overabundance of moisture, which causes stems and leaves to rot.

Those in northern winters may still find species in this list such as sedums and crassulas, as well as other succulents with frost hardiness that defies logic. Although this list of plants has been tested and widely accepted as our most fire resistant plants, other less common succulents are no doubt quite capable of resisting flames so long as they are sufficiently watered. Perhaps the greatest difficulty is finding these plants to buy. Many are easily rooted from cuttings, and a single plant can be propagated into a large colony in a fairly short time. You should be able to obtain most of them by placing a special order at a local nursery or contacting the mail order sources in the resources section of this book.

Group I Plant List

Note: Plants listed may show greater or lesser tolerance of frost depending on site.

Botanical Name	Common Name	Form	Degrees F
Aeonium decorum	–	small shrub	25
Aeonium simsii	–	mounding	25
Agave victoriae-reginae	–	small clump	30
Aloe aristata	–	small clump	33
Aloe brevifolia	–	small clump	33
Carpobrontus edulis	Tottentot Fig	groundcover	25
Crassula lactea	–	groundcover	25
Crassula multicava	–	groundcover	25
Crassula tetragona	–	groundcover	25
Delosperma 'Alba'	White Trailing Iceplant	groundcover	25
Drosanthemum floribundum	Rosea Iceplant	groundcover	25
Drosanthemum hispidum	Rosea Iceplant	groundcover	25
Lampranthus aurantiacus	Bush Iceplant	groundcover	25
Lampranthus filicaulis	Redondo Creeper	groundcover	25
Lampranthus spectabilis	Trailing Iceplant	groundcover	25
Malephora crocea	Iceplant	groundcover	20

Malephora luteola	Yellow Trailing Iceplant	groundcover	30
Portulacaria afra	Elephant's Food	low shrub	30
Sedum acre	Goldmoss Sedum	groundcover	10
Sedum album	Green Stonecrop	groundcover	25
Sedum confusum	–	groundcover	25
Sedum rubrotinctum	Pork and Beans	mounding	25
Senecio mandraliscae	Blue Iceplant	groundcover	25

FIRESCAPING TIP

Iceplant common names often include the descriptive term "trailing." These can be encouraged to cascade off retaining walls, over boulders, railroad ties, and even hang off nearly vertical cliffs if they are given a good planting area at the top. Few, however, are able to gain a foothold on slopes over 30 percent. Rely upon them to protect the soil surface from mild erosion, but their root systems are not extensive enough to prevent large-scale slope failures.

A familiar succulent not listed is Sempervivum tectorum, *commonly called "Hens and Chickens." It shows just how attractive succulents can be when combined with gravel mulches and landscape boulders.*

Group II Moderate Fire Resistance

The plants classified in this group are the most fire resistant non-succulent species. They are primarily herbaceous, with leaves that retain a high moisture content. This, along with low growing habits, increases fire resistance, but every one of these qualities depends on maintenance.

Many of those in group II are vigorous groundcovers and vines that display a strong tendency to accumulate dry, dead, woody twigs and stems beneath the actively growing foliage. If these hidden nests of fuel are not removed, homeowners may have a false sense of security as they see only the green leaves and not the tinder-dry fuel underneath. Although salt bush has proven quite fire resistant, it is notorious for building up large mounds of flammable twigs and stems. A prolonged dry period not only reduces moisture content of the foliage, it also stimulates dieback, which increases this tendency to accumulate volatile material.

Plants in this group offer us a much wider choice of species to work into a design. Although the prostrate growth habits are a single trait they all have in common, there is great diversity of foliage texture and color. Flower size, color, and season of bloom also varies so that the landscape may provide interest year around. Most plants are widely used in California landscaping and easily recognizable. Pay close at-

▲▲▲

Herbs for Firescaping

There are some plants in groups II and III that are classified as herbs. Some are culinary while others are suitable for crafts, potpourri, and interior decorating, thus adding a new dimension to firescaping concepts. This bonus provides an excuse to frequently harvest the herbal foliage because plants in firescaping bands must be trimmed and thinned out frequently.

Group II herbs:

Achillea tomentosa–Wooly Yarrow

Artemisia caucasica–Caucasian Sagebrush, Silver Spreader

Salvia sonomensis–Creeping Sage

Santolina chamaecyparissus–Lavender Cotton

Thymus praecox arcticus (serphyllum)–Mother of Thyme

Group III herbs:

Rosmarinus officinalis 'Prostratus'–Dwarf Rosemary

▲▲▲

tention to their frost tolerances because ivy geranium, for example, is a summer annual in Northern California and may only be permanent on the south coast.

Since it takes a large number of plants to fill in a sizeable ground-cover patch, the most inexpensive means of purchasing them is in flats. The flat is a tray in which a large number of rooted cuttings are grown. You will pay a single price for the entire flat. Some nurseries sell these same plants singly in liners or one-gallon pots. Since a one-gallon plant costs up to five dollars to buy, you are basically paying that price per plant. A flat may cost twelve dollars and contain forty rooted cuttings of the same species, so it's easy to see the savings with flatted plants. If your nursery doesn't have flats of the plant you are looking for, ask them to special order them for you.

One fault of some groundcovers is that they tend to mature and fill in the spaces, then die out in spots as the stems become woody and cease to produce new foliage at the previous rate. *Osteospermum*, the trailing South African daisy, was once the darling of Los Angeles freeway land-scapers, but it was abandoned after early stands began to display this die-out tendency. Other plants that have a tendency to suffer from this aging problem include trailing gazania and ivy geranium.

Many of these group II plants can be established on steep slopes averaging about 30 to 60 percent, but not all root very deeply. Those most reliable and suitable for erosion control are *Euonymus fortunei radicans*, *Myoporum parvifolium prostrata*, *Vinca major*, and *Vinca minor*.

Irrigation for these spreading perennial groundcovers should be a major concern so they do not become overdry and lose their fire-resistant qualities. Ideally this should be done by blanket coverage of a standard spray irrigation system if you have a reliable and extensive water supply. But highly efficient low-pressure systems are more realistic for homes dependent on municipal water supplies. These are the types of plants that have many individuals so that typical drip systems are not feasible. A large number of microspray heads can be used, but they get in the way and make it difficult to mow. If you aren't planning to mow, microspray may be more reasonable, but because regular cleaning and thinning of fuel is required, you may find the myriad hoses and heads a nuisance.

One option is to investigate other products such as leaky pipe, which is a flexible water line that actually "sweats" beads of water along its entire length. New products are being developed all the time, and if you plan to take full advantage of the colorful flowers and foliage variety of these perennial groundcovers to spice up your firescape, it's best to consult an irrigation expert. He or she will be able to explain the most recent technology and products for efficient water delivery. This is even more important when you are planting slopes that require erosion control. Water behaves differently on sloping ground, and an irrigation designer knows how to compensate for the problems of rapid runoff and slow water absorption into the soil.

Group II Plant List
Plants With Moderate Fire Resistance

Botanical Name	Common Name	Exposure	Color	Growth Habit	Comments
Achillea tomentosa	Wooly Yarrow	Sun	Yellow	Mat	Spacing: 6-12" Hardy to 20 F Mow after bloom
Ajuga reptans	Carpet Bugle	Shade	Blue	Mat	Spacing: 6-12" Hardy to 0 F with dieback Mow after bloom
Arctotheca calendula	Cape Weed	Sun	Yellow	Mat	Spacing: 12-18" Frost tender Rapid growth Drought tolerant Erosion control Mowable Resprouts
Artemisia caucasica	Caucasian Sagebrush	Sun	Cream	Mounding	Spacing: 24" Hardy to 10 F Drought tolerant Aromatic
Atriplex cuneata	—	Sun	None	Mounding	Spacing: 30" Hardy to 20 F Drought and salt tolerant Erosion control
Atriplex gardneri	Gardner's Saltbush	Sun	None	Mounding	Spacing: 36" Hardy to 20 F Drought and salt tolerant Erosion control
Atriplex semibaccata	Creeping Australian Saltbush	Sun	None	Mounding	Spacing: 36-50" Hardy to 25 F Drought and salt tolerant Small red fruits Resprouts

Botanical Name	Common Name	Exposure	Color	Growth Habit	Comments
Cerastium tomentosum	Snow in Summer	Sun	White	Small spreading	Spacing: 18-24" Hardy to 20 F Shortlived
Euonymous fortunei radicans	Wintercreeper	Any	None	Spreading	Spacing: 30" Hardy below 0 F Fall foliage color Durable
Fragaria chiloensis	Wild Strawberry	Pt sh.	White	Spreading	Spacing: 12-18" Hardy to 20 F Fast growth Mowable Full sun on coast
Gazania leucolaena	Trailing Gazania	Sun	Yellow	Spreading	Spacing: 18-24" Hardy to 25 F+ − Fast growth Drought tolerant Invasive
Lonicera japonica 'Halliana'	Hall's Honey-suckle	Sun	Yellow/ white	Vine	Spacing: 36"+ Hardy to 0 F Fast growth Fragrant Erosion control
Myoporum parvifolium prostrata		Sun	White	Spreading	Spacing: 36" Hardy to 25 F Fast growth Drought and salt tolerant
Osteospermum fruticosum	Trailing African Daisy	Sun	White/ purple	Spreading	Spacing: 24" Hardy to 25 F Fast growth Erosion control Patchy dieout Resprouts
Pelargonium peltatum	Ivy Geranium	Sun	Many	Spreading	Spacing: 15-18" Frost tender 30 F Fast growth
Phyla nodiflora	−	Sun	Lilac	Mat	Spacing: 12-15" Hardy to 0 F Fast growth Heat tolerant
Potentilla verna	Spring Cinquefoil	Sun/part sh.	Yellow	Mat	Spacing: 12" Hardy to 5 F

Botanical Name	Common Name	Exposure	Color	Growth Habit	Comments
Salvia sonomensis	Creeping Sage	Sun	Blue	Spreading mat	Spacing: 24" Hardy to 0 F Drought tolerant Aromatic Resprouts
Santolina chamae cyparissus	Lavender Cotton	Sun	Yellow	Mounds	Spacing: 30" Hardy to 15 F Drought tolerant Aromatic
Santolina virens	Green Lavender Cotton	Sun	Yellow/green	Mounds	Spacing: 30" Hardy to 15 F Drought tolerant Aromatic Fast growing Resprouts
Thymus praecox-arcticus	Mother of Thyme	Sun	Mauve	Mat	Spacing: 6-12" Hardy to 20 F Aromatic
Thymus pseudolanugi-nosus	Wooly Thyme	Sun	Light pink	Mat	Spacing: 6-12" Hardy to 25 F Aromatic
Verbena peruviana	Peruvian Verbena	Sun	Red	Spreading	Spacing: 12-24" Hardy to 10 F Fast growing Mowable
Vinca major	Periwinkle	Sun/shade	Blue	Spreading	Spacing: 18-24" Hardy to 0 F Fast growing Erosion control Mowable Resprouts
Vinca minor	Dwarf Periwinkle	Part sh.	Blue	Spreading	Spacing:12-18" Hardy to 0 F Fast growing Erosion control Mowable Resprouts

Notes:
1. All spacings are measured from the center of one plant to the center of the next.
2. Plant height indicators: mat=lowest 0-6" spreading=intermediate 6-12" mounding=shrublike 12-18".
3. Degree of hardiness will vary somewhat with each site.

▲▲

Mowable Groundcovers in Groups II and III

Some of the groundcover plants in these two lists are described as mowable. This means you can renew the stand by mowing with a rotary lawn mower set at the highest setting. For very steep, rocky, or irregular surfaces, use a string trimmer. It is important the clippings be removed either with a catcher, or by raking after cutting. If left behind they will dry out and become dangerous fuel. In California, groundcovers are mowed either after blooming or during late winter. Mowing is a good way to get rid of any frost-deadened or discolored leaves and stems. It also helps to remove stems that have become overly woody so that new, succulent ones will grow and support a greater abundance of healthy leaves and flowers. For many gardeners mowing is the easiest way to remove all the faded flowers of matlike groundcovers like cape weed. Some of the best candidates for mowing are hypericum and dwarf vinca.

This example of Hypericum calycinum *"Creeping St. Johnswort" obtains this manicured appearance in the spring following a fall or winter mowing. Foliage is succulent and evenly colored and more likely to bloom.*

▲▲

Group III Lower Fire Resistance

Most of the plants in this list are low-growing woody shrubs, which include many California native species. Their leaves tend to be leathery and dry; naturally reluctant to give up moisture under extreme heat or drought conditions. This characteristic makes them equally as unwilling to lose their hoarded moisture under the dehydrating temperatures of a oncoming fire. The plant's natural, prostrate habits also leave very little fuel volume to feed the flames.

Among these species are some of the best drought-tolerant plants grown today. They are both attractive and durable, yet gardeners everywhere struggle to keep them healthy. Like most California native shrubs, they expect long, hot, dry summers with little water, followed by a rainy, wet winter when they do much of their growing. In the heat of summer, plants survive by slowing down their water needs and becoming partially dormant. Watering during summer should be restricted to infrequent but deep irrigations, much like an occasional summer thunderstorm cloudburst.

The chief enemy is poor drainage causing wet roots, which doesn't often occur on slopes, so plants growing there will need more water during the spring, summer, and fall. On flat, soggy, or very low ground, beware of when and how much water is applied. Manzanita and ceanothus are both notoriously finicky about water out of season or poor drainage in general, so plant them with care.

Baccharis or coyote bush has been planted extensively on freeway embankments throughout California. There it displays a typical characteristic of creeping shrubs as they age. Because the plant is supported by a stubby upright woody stem that radiates out with branches in different directions, there is great tension upon this central point called the crown. When the plant gets old, the main branches that have developed into large limbs of foliage pull away from the crown. If they do not break off (these plants tend to be brittle), their foliage falls away to expose the crown. Direct summer sun upon this central stem causes it to

FIRESCAPING TIP

It's best to plant most of these species during the fall and not in spring. Fall is when natives are gearing up for their growing season, so transplants will be active enough to resist transplant shock, and are assured a long, cool growing season to become established. This allows the plant to send its roots out of the pot-shaped root ball and into native soil. There they are more likely to find deeply trapped moisture when the heat and dryness of summer approaches. To save yourself lots of money and dead, highly stressed plants, plant your firescape in the fall.

dry and eventually split apart, which signals a decline in the lifespan of the plant. On those freeway plantings you'll see this splitting apart, and if you look closely there's a good view of dense, twiggy growth underneath. Instead of moaning about the rush-hour traffic, begin to study the freeway embankment plantings. There your observations will show you how iceplant, coyote bush, trailing African daisy, and English ivy behave in mass plantings over the long term.

You can discourage this weight and splitting of creeping shrubs by judicious pruning beginning the first year. The goal is to balance the plant and discourage one branch from growing on top of another. The top branch uses the bottom one as a trellis, denying it light and causing defoliation. Meanwhile the top branch is growing beautifully, gaining new leaves every day to make it heavier. Eventually the bottom branch breaks or collapses from the weight. The top branch never developed a strong stem due to the natural trellis, so when burdened with its own weight it falls outward away from the crown to expose it. If there is enough weight, this heavy branch will pull against that of branches on the opposite side of the crown and split the plant in half. Visualize this scenario whenever you are pruning to maintain the health and fire-resistant qualities of these creeping shrubs.

Group III Plant List

Plants With Low Fire Resistance

Botanical Name	Common Name	Exposure	Flowers	Growth Habit	Comments
Arctostaphylos hookeri 'Monterey Carpet'	Monterey Manzanita	Sun	Pink	Creeping shrub	Spacing: 3' Hardy to 15 F Drought tolerant Slow growing
Arctostaphylos uva-ursi	Bearberry	Sun	Pink	Creeping shrub	Spacing: 3' Hardy to 20 F+ − Drought tolerant Slow growing Red berries
Arctostaphylos uva-ursi 'Point Reyes'	Point Reyes Manzanita	Sun	Pink	Creeping shrub	Spacing: 3' Hardy to 20F+ − Drought tolerant Slow growing
Baccharis pilularis prostrata	Dwarf Coyote Bush	Sun	None	Mounding shrub	Spacing: 30" Hardy to 10 F Drought tolerant Erosion control

Botanical Name	Common Name	Exposure	Flowers	Growth Habit	Comments
Baccharis pilularis 'Twin Peaks'	Coyote Bush Hybrid	Sun	None	Mounding shrub	Spacing: 30" Hardy to 10 F Drought tolerant Erosion Control Resprouts
Carissa grandiflora 'Green Carpet'	Natal Plum	Sun	White	Mounding shrub	Spacing: 40" Hardy to 20 F Spines Fragrant flowers Edible red fruit
Ceanothus gloriosus	Point Reyes Ceanothus	Sun	Blue	Creeping shrub	Spacing: 4' Hardy to 20 F Drought tolerant
Ceanothus griseus horizontalis	Carmel Creeper	Sun	Blue	Creeping shrub	Spacing: 5' Hardy to 20 F Drought tolerant
Ceanothus prostratus	Squaw Carpet	Sun	Blue	Creeping shrub	Spacing: 4' Hardy below 0 F (mountain elevations) Drought tolerant
Cistus crispus	–	Sun	Violet	Creeping shrub	Spacing: 30" Hardy to 15 F Drought tolerant Erosion control
Cistus salviifolius	Sageleaf Rockrose	Sun	White	Creeping shrub	Spacing: 40" Hardy to 15 F Drought tolerant Erosion control
Hedera canariensis	Algerian Ivy	Pt Sun	None	Spreading	Spacing: 14" Hardy to 20 F Erosion control Mowable Resprouts
Hedera helix	English Ivy	Pt Sun	None	Spreading	Spacing: 14" Hardy to below 0 F Erosion control Mowable
Helianthemum nummularium	Sunrose	Sun	Multi	Mounding perennial	Spacing: 18" Hardy to 20 F Drought tolerant Erosion control Short lived

Botanical Name	Common Name	Exposure	Flowers	Growth Habit	Comments
Hypericum calycinum	Aaron's Beard	Sun	Yellow	Spreading	Spacing: 12" Hardy to 0 F Erosion control Mowable Resprouts
Lantana montevidensis	Trailing Lantana	Sun	Purple	Spreading	Spacing: 18" Hardy to 30+ − Mowable
Rosmarinus officinalis 'Prostratus'	Dwarf Rosemary	Sun	Blue	Mounding perennial	Spacing: 18" Hardy to 15 F Drought/wind tolerant Erosion control Culinary herb
Teucrium chamaedrys	Germander	Sun	Purple	Mounding perennial	Spacing: 12" Hardy to 0 F Drought tolerant Erosion control

Garden Qualities of Group I, II, & III Plants

Note: Spp. indicates all species of this genus listed in above groups.

California Natives
Arctostaphylos spp.–Manzanita
Baccharis spp.–Coyote Bush
Ceanothus spp.–California Lilac
Salvia sonomensis–Creeping Sage

Masses of Flower Color
Achillea tomentosa–Wooly Yarrow
Arctotheca calendula–Cape Weed
Ceanothus spp.–California Lilac
Cerastium tomentosum–Snow in Summer
Gazania leucolaena–Trailing Gazania
Hypericum calycinum–Aaron's Beard
Lantana montevidensis–Trailing Lantana
Osteospermum fruticosum–Trailing African Daisy
Malephora luteola–Yellow Trailing Iceplant
Pelargonium peltatum–Ivy Geranium
Verbena peruviana–Peruvian Verbena
Iceplants: *Carpobrotus, Delosperma, Drosanthemum* spp., *Lampranthus* spp., *Malephora* spp.

Erosion Control

Arctotheca calendula–Cape Weed
Atriplex spp.–Saltbush
Baccharis spp.–Coyote Bush
Cistus spp.–Rockrose
Hedera spp.–Ivy
Hypericum calycinum–Aaron's Beard
Rosmarinus officinalis 'Prostratus'–Creeping Rosemary
Teucrium chamaedrys–Germander

Drought Tolerant

Arctostaphylos spp.–Manzanita
Artemesia caucasica–Caucasian Sagebrush
Atriplex spp.–Saltbush
Baccharis spp.–Coyote Bush
Ceanothus spp.–California Lilac
Cistus spp.–Rockrose
Hypericum calycinum–Aaron's Beard
Euonymus fortunei radicans–Wintercreeper
Lantana montevidensis–Trailing Lantana
Lonicera japonica 'Halliana'–Hall's Honeysuckle
Myoporum parvifolium prostrata
Rosmarinus officinalis 'Prostratus'–Creeping Rosemary
Salvia sonomensis–Creeping Sage
Santolina spp.–Lavender Cotton
Teucrium chamaedrys–Germander

▲▲▲

Selected California Native Flowers for Firescape Bands

The chief qualities of all fire-resistant plants include high moisture content and low fuel volumes. For dry gardens where plant selection is limited by frost or lack of irrigation water, the regimen of the above lists may be broken with some bright color of native wildflowers. But consider only those species which are very low-growing and tolerant of being cut back on a regular basis. Keep in mind that not all species of lupine, for example, are low-growing, but there are some good short annual varieties that can be seen blanketing the dry gravel shoulders of many California roadsides. California poppy is naturally low-growing and perfect for spotting in color. Large quantities of seed for both dwarf lupines and poppies as well

This is Applewood Seed Company's low-growing mixture *of wildflowers, which grow no more than sixteen inches tall. Flowers can be mowed after blooming season finishes in early summer. A super-short mixture is also available with wildflower species that grow no taller than ten inches. Both are perfect for adding seasonal color to outer firescape zones.*

as other ground-hugging wildflowers can be obtained through the wildflower seed sources in the back of the book.

Two of California's most attractive shrubby perennials, California fuchsia and monkey flower, both add interest to firescape bands, and if kept neatly pruned, present very low fuel volumes. Our native fuchsia offers potently colored lipstick-red flowers that attract hummingbirds. The soft apricot blossoms of monkey flower are a bit more finicky as they grow upon very steep rocky cliffs in foothill regions. Both plants rarely exceed a foot tall, but may spread out in diameter as they age. These two should be purchased as plants in one-gallon containers because they do not readily grow from seed.

Eschscholzia californica–California Poppy

Lupinus sp.–Dwarf Lupine

Mimulus sp.–Monkey Flower

Zauschneria–California Fuchsia

▲▲▲

Other Plants for Fire Bands

There are many other attractive landscape plants that may be combined with those of groups I, II, and III. These are primarily groundcovers and very small or low-growing perennials. They may have been omitted from the above groups for different reasons. Some simply haven't been tested. Others were not available where, or when, the testing was done. Still more do not show fire-resistant characteristics, but qualify due to a naturally low fuel volume and prostrate growth habits.

Hybrid clumping gazanias can be a perfect firescape accent perennial. Strains offer intensely colored flowers from white to deep red and many hues in between. They are rugged and durable but should not be considered long-lived, nor do they spread like trailing gazania (Gazania leucolaena) *in the Group II plant list.*

In order to increase the choice of plants for firescapes, consider these an optional group for accent color or for substitutes when other plants aren't available. They will require the same attention to detail in maintenance in order to keep fuel to a minimum and plants fully hydrated by regular irrigation. Do not plant them in masses, for this provides long avenues of unbroken fuels. Spot them in as singles, or in small, widely spaced groups. Annuals should be removed entirely after they go to seed or when their stems become overly dry. The list below are some common garden annuals and perennials that will add seasonal color to firescapes, especially in the band closest to the house where flowers are most appreciated.

Group IV Plant List

Plants With Low Growth Habits But Not Fire Resistant

Some of these plants are true groundcovers while others make colorful accents for interest and diversity in fire bands. Rarely grow taller than 12–18" and all are perennial.

Botanical Name	Common Name	Exposure	Color	Growth Habit	Comments
Agapanthus africanus 'Peter Pan'	Dwarf Lily of the Nile	Sun/Pt Shade	Blue	Tufts	Spacing: 18" Hardy to 20 F Strap-leafed
Armeria maritima	Thrift, Sea Pink	Sun/Pt Shade	Pink	Small tufts	Spacing: 12" Hardy to 0 F
Anthemis nobilis	Camomile	Sun	White	Spreading	Spacing: 6"-12" Hardy to 10 F Mowable
Campanula poscharskyana	Serbian Bellflower	Pt. Shade	Blue/	Spreading	Spacing: 6-12" Hardy to 0 F Mowable
Coprosma prostrata	–	Pt. Shade	–	Spreading	Spacing: 24" Hardy to 30 F
Gazania splendens	Clumping Gazania	Sun	Many	Small mounds	Spacing: 12" Hardy to 25 F Short-lived
Herniaria glabra	Green Carpet	Sun	–	Mat	Spacing: 6" Hardy to 20 F Succulent
Isotoma fluviatilis	Blue Star Creeper	Sun	Blue	Mat	Spacing: 6-12" Hardy to 25 F
Liriope 'Silvery Sunproof'	–	Pt. Shade	Purple	Small tufts	Spacing: 12" Hardy to 25 F Strap-leafed
Ophiopogon japonicum	Mondo Grass	Pt. Shade	–	Small tufts	Spacing: 6-8" Hardy to 20 F Strap-leafed

Annuals and Perennials for Firescapes

Alyssum saxatile–Basket of Gold
Bellis perennis–English Daisy
Dianthus–China Pinks
Coreoposis auriculata nana–
    Dwarf Coreopsis

Heuchera sanguinea–Coral Bells
Iberis sempervirens–Candytuft
Lobelia erinus–Annual Lobelia
Vinca rosea–Dwarf Periwinkle

Two low-growing perennials for firescaping that make nice neat little mounds and flower profusely. The white blossoms are candytuft (Iberis sempervirens), *and the others are China pinks, which are also available in many different flower colors. Both plants can have the spent blooms easily cut back at the end of the season with hedge clippers.*

Trees in Fire Bands

Just because there are no trees in the three fire-resistant plant groups doesn't mean there cannot be trees in a firescape. Trees provide shade, habitat, and privacy and improve the visual quality of a homesite. The key is knowing which ones to plant, where to put them within fire bands, and how to calculate proper spacings. Whenever possible keep them outside of zone 1, but if they must be close to the house be sure you select a very small, slow-growing species. The further trees are away from the house the safer your site will be.

Not all trees are equally vulnerable to fire. It is well known that deciduous trees are more capable of resisting fire because they contain greater amounts of moisture, and when dormant and leafless there is far less fuel volume available. Ornamental varieties of deciduous or *broadleaf* evergreen trees closer to the house should be small in stature so fuel volumes are kept to a minimum. Of these, species with thick, succulent, and leathery leaves are the best choices, but they must be sufficiently irrigated to retain these qualities. Those that shed large amounts of leaves or peeling bark as well as other types of flammable litter are undesirable.

Conifers are evergreens that have needles instead of leaves. Typical examples are pine, juniper, and cypress. They contain oils and pitch that are extremely volatile, particularly when plants are desiccated and suffering from drought conditions. Other trees such as the eucalyptus and acacia are loaded with similar oils, which contributed to the difficulties in the Berkeley Hills fire where these species were plentiful and very dry due to prolonged drought.

Trees also have another role in firescapes. Many with large root systems have been planted on hillsides to stabilize soil. If these trees are burned, their roots are still effective for erosion control and will usually resprout from the stumps. Good choices for slopes are coast live oak (*Quercus agrifolia*), valley oak (*Quercus lobata*), alder (*Alnus rhombifolia* or *Alnus cordata*), and sycamore (*Platanus racemosus*).

There is information in the preceding chapter about thinning existing trees within fire bands. This applies primarily to native stands where species is predetermined by the ecosystem. But if you have the choice of whether or not to plant trees, it's best to keep them widely spaced, and as far apart as you can manage. Burning trees produce flames sometimes twice as high as their crowns, which can send the fire towering over your rooftop.

You may be faced with the dilemma of shade verses fire safety. Shade trees reduce energy consumption (air conditioner), limit reflected heat from paving and bare ground, and make outdoor living possible in the hot summer months. Here lies the dilemma, which can only be re-

FIRESCAPING TIP

Some species of shrubs and groundcovers also have the ability to resprout almost immediately after a fire, when encouraged by regular irrigation or rainfall. For very steep sites with heavy dependance on vegetation to hold the slope, this ability is critical to soil stabilization. Incorporating these species into firescape slope planting insures that there will be a network of living roots to hold the soil even though the aboveground portions have been burned off. Keep in mind that an extremely intense fire may ultimately kill the plants, but the lower fuel volumes in a firescape may slow the fire down enough to help the plants survive. Look for the term "resprouts" in the fire-resistant plant lists to find ones with this unique quality.

solved by taking into consideration site factors such as slope and exposure while evaluating the potential vulnerability to fires. With luck you will find a balance, which allows for a few carefully placed shade trees at the appropriate spacing.

In terms of native trees and as a model for shade trees, there should be a minimum of 10 feet from the edge of the canopy of one tree to that of the next on level or gently sloping ground. For greater slopes this may be 20 or 30 feet depending on the exact percentages. This dimension is based upon the canopy limits of a *mature* tree, so when planning use of ornamental trees choose and locate them according to their ultimate sizes.

Small Trees for California Firescapes
(Frost tolerance varies.)
Acer palmatum–Japanese Maple
Ficus benjamina–Chinese Banyan
Lagerstroemia indica–Crape Myrtle
Maytenus boaria–Mayten Tree

Deciduous Shade Trees for California Firescapes
(All acceptable as urban street trees.)
Alnus cordata–Italian Alder
Ginkgo biloba–Maidenhair Tree
Liquidambar styraciflua–American Sweet Gum
Liriodendron tulipifera–Tulip Tree
Pistacia chinensis–Chinese Pistache
Prunus cerasifera 'Atropurpurea'–Flowering Plum
Pyrus calleryana 'Bradford'–Bradford Pear

Arranging Fire Band Plants

One basic rule of all planting design is to use a variety of species rather than just one or two plant types. This insures that if a disease or pest strikes one variety of plant, the entire stand will not be destroyed. Another concept is to prioritize plants, which becomes helpful if water rationing may occur in the future. A core group of durable and drought-tolerant spreading shrubs could make up the majority of the area, but interspersed could be annual flowers or other colorful accents and groundcover plants. Under rationing, this core group would be spared at all costs while the rest could be allowed to die out.

The heights and fuel volume of firescaping plants will vary according to how well they are pruned and maintained. Although all are low growing, you can create variety and take advantage of the growth

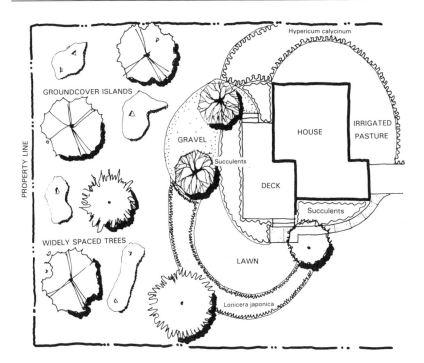

GROUNDCOVER ISLANDS

PROPERTY LINE

Hypericum calycinum

GRAVEL

Succulents

HOUSE

IRRIGATED PASTURE

DECK

Succulents

WIDELY SPACED TREES

LAWN

Lonicera japonica

Sample Firescape Plan

This plan incorporates many of the plants and concepts of firescaping. Irrigated pasture and lawn provide plenty of green around the house while succulents are the only plants contacting the building walls. Outside are long bands of groundcovers and some widely spaced, small accent trees. The peripheral area is planted with drip-irrigated groundcover islands and shade trees. The remainder of the ground plan can be planted in annual grasses and/or wildflowers that die out at the end of spring and may be mowed short for minimal fuel availability and no watering requirements.

FIRESCAPING TIP

If you are not familiar with plants, it's worth the money to hire a professional landscape designer or landscape architect to prepare a planting plan for you. Using the concepts and plant lists in this book, the designer will be able to discuss what the final product will look like and may even sketch it out in perspective. A skilled horticulturist is also helpful when blending native ecosystems with ornamental plants, which is a tricky venture when dealing with oaks and other sensitive Californians that do not always tolerate root disturbance or unseasonable irrigation water.

Crushed white granite gravel has been used in this modest planting showing wide spacing beneath neatly trimmed shrubs. The natural coloring of the gravel is attractive with the deep green foliage plant. The mayten tree (Maytenus boaria) is slow-growing and remains small when mature.

Although not fire resistant, this attractive little California garden relies on gravel and other creative pavings that blend naturally into the landscape. The plants are mostly low-growing species of heather, which bloom in intensely bright colors around Labor Day. If treated like low hedges and sheared back each year they can retain low fuel volumes.

Here large, flat stones have been incorporated into a rock garden landscape, which relies on river-rounded gravels to add texture to the ground plant. Very low-growing, matlike groundcovers will eventually fill in between each of the large stones for a lush, carpeted effect with little to no fuel at all. (Design: Susan Elmore.)

Another view of the same garden showing how thrift and other low-growing flowering perennials and groundcovers coupled with attractive lighting fixtures, soft mounds of soil, boulders, and a dwarf tree results in a very low-fuel-volume, high-visual-quality landscape. (Design: Susan Elmore.)

habits by planting the taller varieties behind the shorter ones whenever possible. Intermix plants by arranging very small masses of each type rather than a hodgepodge of individuals. Let these drifts stand out from one another by contrasting flower color, foliage, and irregular textures. They can even be separated by narrow gravel walkways to increase their visual impact. The more graceful your hand in selecting and locating your plants, the greater sense of unity the planting will display while still retaining sufficient diversity.

Many rural homesites, farms and ranches are blessed with high-producing wells or irrigation water supplies. In these cases one of the most productive types of firescape techniques can be implemented: the irrigated pasture. This is simply an open space planted with a standard mixture of deep-rooted orchard grasses and a variety of clovers. Where there is livestock, this fire band becomes an agricultural crop for grazing and may even support deer and elk as well.

A larger homesite can be fire resistant by design. For example, a defensible home can be surrounded by irrigated pasture with just a few trees, and these may be kept clean of ladder fuels by nibbling horses or cows. Perhaps the driveway is routed around the house so it becomes a fire band free of any fuel at all. Corrals and ponds also offer excellent opportunities for home protection.

Risky Business: Volatile Landscape Plants to Avoid

Acacia spp.	Acacia
Cedrus spp.	Cedar
Cupressus spp.	Cypress
Dodonaea spp.	Hopseed Bush
Eucalyptus spp.	Eucalyptus
Juniperus spp.	Juniper
Pennisetum spp.	Fountain Grass
Pinus spp.	Pines
Bougainvillea	Bougainvillea
Phormium tenax	New Zealand Flax
Cortaderia selloana	Pampas Grass
Gelsemium sempervirens	Carolina Jessamine
Hakea suaveolens	Hakea
All ornamental grasses	
All berry vines	

7

▲▲▲▲▲▲▲▲▲▲▲▲▲▲▲ ▲▲▲▲▲▲▲▲▲▲▲▲▲▲▲

Long-Term Maintenance of Plants and Equipment

This is the most important chapter in the book because proper care and upkeep of a firescape and fire fighting systems is critical to whether or not they function when needed. For example, lack of long-term attention can result in fire resistant plants loading up with dead twigs, leaves, and branches to grow into monstrous, yet sometimes invisible fuel volumes. Accumulations of needles and leaves upon a rooftop may transform class B roofing material into a flammable hazard. Rodents in the pump house, earwigs clogging the sprinkler heads, and decaying hoses could seriously disable, if not eliminate, your emergency water supply.

There are four main categories of a proper maintenance program:

1. Care of plants.
2. Fine tuning of irrigation systems.
3. Testing and protection of emergency water supply and delivery systems.
4. Attention to house and outbuildings.

   Each of these categories is equally important because neglect of one may render the others ineffective. For example, if you allow the fireband plants to become overgrown and develop high fuel volumes, your emergency water system may not be capable of resisting the much taller and more intense flames resulting from the additional vegetation.

▲▲

CATEGORY 1 Care of Plants

Plants in firescapes may be comprised of existing native species, ornamental plants, or both. Obviously, plants are unlike a house or other buildings that remain the same over many decades: Every day your trees grow a bit larger, shrubs spread out, and the litter of fallen leaves grows thicker. This is the natural increase of the earth's biomass, which ultimately leads to rising fuel volumes in firescapes unless properly managed.

Regardless of the nature of the vegetation, it's best to think about proper care in terms of fuels and fire types. As detailed in other chapters, fuels occur in three locations and may be either live or dead materials. Surface fires feed off fuels close to the ground. Dead surface fuels

▲▲▲

An Overview of Tasks

There are some basic activities which will be required for management of all firescape plants. Understanding the exact definition of these terms makes the maintenance guidelines in this chapter easier to understand.

Pruning This is the methodical cutting back of plant parts to reduce the overall size, or to remove dead twigs or branches. Also includes thinning of tree canopies and reducing the tops of tall shrubs.

Litter Reduction This activity gathers and removes any unwanted dead materials from the soil surface. It does not apply to decorative mulches.

Weed Control Removal of existing weeds both alive and dead. Includes ground treatments of various types to discourage the growth of any new weeds.

Revegetation Replacement of any plants that have died out in order to reduce soil erosion or for aesthetic purposes.

Mowing Open spaces treated with irrigated pasture, lawn, or when renewing "mowable" groundcovers, cut with a rotary lawn mower on a regular basis and the clippings disposed of. Naturally occurring annual grasses that die out in late spring also require mowing or trimming and chaff removal. Large-scale sites may be cut with a tractor and flail mower. Remember to mow in the morning when grass is still moist.

Removal Elimination of remnants of dead plants, fallen trees, branches, or stumps. Thinning out of living plants that have outgrown space allotted to them.

▲▲▲

include leaves and needles, fallen twigs, cones, and bark. Live surface fuels are comprised of living leaves and needles still attached to plants, low branches, weeds, and other plant material within the first few feet above the ground.

Aerial fuels are mainly living and dead parts of tree tops—the main components of crown fires. Tree canopies too close together provide a clear avenue of fuel. Ladder fuels include tall shrubs or drooping foliage, as well as lower branches that have died back, fallen snags, stumps, and anything else that will provide a "rung in the ladder" upon which a fire rises to tree tops, or drops from the trees down to ground level.

All these factors have been reviewed because they are the reasons why maintenance is required in a fire-resistant landscape. It's easiest to divide tasks according to the fuel types so that you can make the proper decisions as to what must be done, and how frequently the job must be repeated. Because every homesite is different, with varying species and layout, the duties required will vary in kind. An effective maintenance program must be tailored to meet the individual needs of the site.

Management of Ground Fuels

Spring Remove any frost-damaged plants or prune back burned leaves and branches. Control plant heights. Rake up litter caused by winter storms. First mowing of natural grasses. Plant new seed or plants

The annual grass surrounding this well-manicured tree is unirrigated and by late spring is dying out for the summer. It has already been mowed very short with no residual clippings or chaff left behind. This is an example of how natural grasses can remain attractive without watering, and yet offer no fuel to an oncoming fire.

as required for replacement. Renew thinning mulches. Control weeds manually or with herbicide while actively growing. Fertilize.

Summer   Cut back spent flowers. Prune back wayward growth. Second natural grass mowing May–June. Control weeds. Irrigate well.

Fall   Control weeds. Irrigate well. Remove plants going to seed. Rake up fallen autumn leaves. Remove all weeds. Mow if necessary. Replant as needed. Fertilize (optional).

Winter   Prune back summer growth. Burn slash with valid permit. Seed wildflowers and grasses before winter rain. Replant as needed.

Management of Aerial Fuels

This applies to canopies of all trees, evergreen and deciduous. Aerial fuels include both living branches and accumulations of litter such as dead needles still attached or resting on the limbs. Pruning is the main activity, with attention focused on decreasing canopy diameters that may encroach on the open space between each tree. Trees with excessive amounts of branches that create heavy fuel loads must also be

▲▲▲

The Pine Bark Beetle

Pine bark beetles have attacked stands of pine timber throughout the state. The beetles have always been here, but now that trees are stressed by drought the pests are better able to reproduce. They will attack the weakest individuals first, and there are plenty of these since our forests are overcrowded due to the lack of fires in California for nearly a century. The beetles are one of nature's culling mechanisms to weed out weaker trees and keep forests healthy.

The insect invades the trees through the soft growing tip at the very top, which is why trees typically die from the top down, or from side branch tips. Normally there is sufficient water pressure within the trees to exclude the beetles, but prolonged drought has reduced it enough to allow the beetles to enter and lay their eggs. These hatch out into voracious larvae that burrow through the cambium layer beneath the bark, destroying the tree's ability to transport moisture and nutrients. Eventually the larvae mature and pupate into flying adults, which then leave the host tree to lay yet more eggs at the top of the next suitable individual. It is recommended that any trees or tree parts that contain beetle eggs or larvae be burned immediately and not transported elsewhere to further extend the beetle's territory.

▲▲▲

thinned every few years. Canopy reduction, or thinning, is best done in California during the winter and early spring while growth is slower. This is also the wet season, when chain saws are less of a hazard, and where permitted the materials may be immediately burned. A chipper/shredder machine turns this refuse into valuable mulch. Removal of dead limbs in deciduous trees is best done during summer because they are only visible when the tree is fully leafed out.

Ladder Fuels

A well-designed firescape should not have any ladder fuels, but sometimes they gradually develop unnoticed over long periods of time. As trees grow taller, more of the low branches may be pruned away as long as they don't comprise more than one-third of the total height. Taller native shrubs in the outermost band may also gain some height, and if close enough to a tree they could act as ladder fuel. There must be clear space between the top of the shrub and the lowest tree branch. This space should be roughly three times the height of the shrub.

CATEGORY 2   Fine Tuning of Irrigation Systems

There are two reasons why fine tuning of irrigation systems is so important. First, it is the only means of keeping a firescape alive and functional so there is sufficient moisture in the plants for them to resist fire. Second, water is a precious resource in California and should be used as efficiently as possible, not only because it reduces our water bills, but so the system is still able to function under water rationing.

For those using standard irrigation systems, the lines will be underground with only the risers and/or heads visible. The problem that most frequently occurs with these systems is clogged or malfunctioning heads. Clogging can be caused by insects in the lines or particulate matter such as calcium that may break free from the pipes to block the nozzles. Gear-driven or pop-up heads may not operate if grains of soil or other matter become jammed in the mechanism. If heads are bumped they can be forced out of adjustment, delivering water where it is not needed and leaving the intended area partially dry. To insure all the heads are operating properly and there are no underground leaks or cracks, test the system at least four times per year to check coverage and output.

Drip systems are a bit more difficult to check because they have a network of tubing and emitters hidden under plants and mulch. There are dozens of ways tubing can become damaged, and it should be checked for leaks at least four times a year but preferably more often. Emitters can also clog up, and if these are not checked monthly you may never know they are blocked until the plants wilt or die. To reduce clogging use insect-resistant emitters and install a filter on each valve of the system to strain out particulate matter in the water supply. Clean out the filter frequently or it will become full and reduce flow rates.

Microspray tubing is equally as vulnerable but it's easier to check for clogged emitters because the spray heads are visible. These systems also benefit from filters and should be tested and checked frequently. As plants grow larger, it is necessary to reposition the heads to insure adequate coverage. The gradual moisture reduction in your firescape plants from malfunctioning irrigation systems may not be visible until it is too late to quickly rehydrate them again.

CATEGORY 3 Emergency Water Supply and Delivery Systems

Wildfires can start and threaten your homesite in an instant, leaving absolutely no time to fuss with equipment. Discovering your supply line is riddled with holes while a fire is at your doorstep is a deadly serious matter. Ask any professional fire fighter and you may be surprised at how often their hoses are inspected and replaced, just to be sure.

The emergency water reservoir should be well marked so that fire fighters may utilize it when protecting your home. It must be kept full at all times and checked frequently, especially in hot weather. Keeping the water free of debris that might clog the suction hose of a pump is also important. Even if you have a screen on the end of the hose, it can become encased in leaves and the suction will hold the blockage against the screen as long as you are pumping. Clouds or strings of algae can also clog the small screen holes.

Hoses can become a real menace if not properly cared for. They should be reserved exclusively for fire-flow systems and not used in the garden. Keep them in the same location at all times, a place protected from rodents, insects, and both direct sun and winter cold. Coil loosely on a flat, dry surface so there is less tendency for kinking or corkscrew stiffness when in use. Store the nozzles with hoses.

Any roof-watering apparatus constructed out of white PVC pipe should be stored away from direct sunlight. This material is designed to be either buried or used indoors. It will break down if subjected to di-

▲▲

Small Engine Maintenance

Most generators and engine driven water pumps rely on a four-cycle engine. Anyone who has struggled with a reluctant lawn mower knows how temperamental they can be after sitting for awhile. It is essential this equipment is stored properly and operated at regular intervals to insure it functions when needed.

It's a good idea to purchase a book on small gasoline engines for basics on storage and maintenance. One of the primary issues is the fuel itself. Newer gasoline blends tend to contain methanol and other additives that are not good for small engines. Try to buy only name-brand high-octane supreme gas. Gasoline also tends to separate and evaporate leaving sludge if left to sit for any period of time. When the small engine is stored with gas in the fuel tank, fuel lines and carburetor, the sludge is likely to foul the engine or make it hard to start later on.

To be on the safe side, run your generator or pump out of gas after each test or use. Store gas in a separate container and replace the supply every month or two, particularly during fire season. If the engine is needed in an emergency, have a funnel handy so you can fill or refill the tank quickly and fire it up. For electric starting engines, consult the manufacturer regarding storage and specific requirements of the battery. Change the oil in the engine at least once a year.

▲▲

rect sunlight and extremes of temperatures over time. There are no visible signs of weakened PVC except perhaps a slight discoloration, but it will become overly brittle and crack under very little pressure.

CATEGORY 4   House and Outbuildings

This applies not only to your house but to any sheds, barns, stables, garages, or structures of any kind on your property. Even the most fireproof roofing will become volatile if covered with a layer of pine needles or leaves. Keep the roof as clean as possible all year around, and remove debris from rain gutters. The new fascia gutters are deeper than the older styles and a greater quantity of leaves can build up before they become visible at the top. Because rain gutters are rarely in use during fire season, they are often full and hazardous. Although they are not part of the structure, remove all flammable plants or weeds along building foundations.

Other Fire Fighting Equipment

Whether it is you or fire fighters who protect your house, a number of essential tools must be kept at hand. These should be separate from hand tools used for gardening or cleaning. Keep them stored where they will be available at a moment's notice. They include one or more of the following: a large metal bucket, rake, shovel, pruning saw, axe, and lopping shears. A gasoline-operated chainsaw can be helpful as well. Have two or more watertight plastic garbage cans available to fill with water and station at important points around the house if fire threatens. You'll also need a ladder to gain access to your roof, and for larger houses two ladders might be more useful so there is one at either end.

8

What to Do When the Fire Comes

The California Department of Forestry and Fire Protection has created an excellent videotape called "Fire Safe—Inside and Out" which teaches the guidelines detailed in this and other chapters of this book. Inquire about borrowing it from the nearest CDF station. The video is realistic and allows you to see an actual occurrence, which helps to convey the urgency of a fire scene. As in other emergency situations, there will be those who panic, a state which does not lead to making logical decisions during the crucial moments when fire approaches. Above all it is essential to stay calm and attend to the activities necessary to insure the safety of your family and that of your home as well. The key is to have a well-detailed fire plan established *ahead of time* so that each person knows exactly what to do.

Put Together a Survival Pack

Expectant mothers have traditionally packed up important items in an overnight bag well before the delivery date. The bag is ready to go at a moment's notice. Preparing for a fire is done much the same way because if you must evacuate suddenly, which often occurs during wildfires, everything will be ready to make this difficult situation less frantic. In fact, it's also a good idea in case of a house fire as well. There are two groups of items that should be considered. First there are the basic necessities such as a change of clothes, medicines, cosmetics, a coat, list of important phone numbers, and other essential items. For those living in remote or rural areas, the list is even more essential because goods and services will not be close by.

A Survival Evacuation Pack

1. **Leather hiking boots with heavy soles** Synthetic materials may melt in hot ash.
2. **Flashlight with fresh batteries** Replace batteries annually or include second set.
3. **Canteen** Keep it full of water if you live far from any rivers, lakes, or other water sources. Use a large one to be sure there is sufficient water to wet your clothing as well as for drinking.
4. **Large cotton bandanna** It can be soaked in water and tied around your nose and mouth to filter smoke. Synthetic fibers are less absorbent and may melt.
5. **Heavy, long-sleeved shirt** Thickly woven wool or cotton, which may be soaked to better insulate against heat and resist embers.
6. **High-energy snack foods** These are found in all survival packages and will keep indefinitely in original containers. Chocolate, granola bars, trail mix, etc.
7. **Lightweight, compact first aid kit** Include a supply of important prescription medications.
8. **Rescue location aids** A metal whistle and neck lanyard for location by ground searchers. 6 by 6-foot square of fluorescent orange nylon helps to locate you from the air.

▲▲

Wildfire Tip

Whenever there is a natural disaster, telephone communication may be cut off and your radio may be the only means of keeping in touch with the size of a wildfire and in which direction it is likely to move. The best way to be well informed both while at home and after evacuation is through a hand-held radio scanner with both police and radio frequencies. You will know exactly what fire fighting agencies and police are doing at all times. Be sure to keep fresh batteries with the scanner and a spare set for backup. You can also listen to it during fire weather to keep up on smaller brush fires that inevitably pop up at this time of year. Radio Shack and other retail electronics stores offer reasonably priced models.

▲▲

9. **Construction hard hat**   Protects your hair from hot embers that fill the skies in all wildfires. Protects against head injuries in forests where there is the risk of falling branches or even entire trees.

10. **A sturdy backpack**   If you must travel for a long distance, having all these items in a comfortable backpack is a lifesaver, particularly when both hands must be free to climb steep terrain.

Homesite Survival Tips

If there is a fire in your area, utility lines and telephone poles are often burned. Although your house may not be threatened, if the lines supporting your services are cut, you may be without power for some time. Survival during and after a fire may also mean you must be able to function without water or electrical supplies. This is also helpful in case of earthquake. The CDF suggests each house be equipped with the following:

1. **Three-day supply of food** sufficient for the entire family; foods that do not require refrigeration or cooking and will store indefinitely.

2. **Three-day supply of drinking water** can be stored prebottled or in thoroughly cleaned and sealed gallon milk jugs, water cooler, or plastic liter bottles.

3. **Assortment of survival aids** such as a portable radio, flashlight, extra batteries, emergency cooking equipment, fuel, and portable lantern.

4. **First aid kit and medical supplies.**

Preparing to Evacuate

Fires never occur when expected and often families are fragmented, with adults in one place and one or more of the children somewhere else. It is important that everyone understands there is a second location where all are to meet up eventually. This may be the home of a relative or close friend within a few miles from home.

The sudden order to evacuate leaves many homeowners in a quandary as to which of their cherished possessions to load into the car. Consider keeping some of them permanently in a safe deposit box or fireproof safe to reduce the number of things to take away during evacuation. The confusion around fires can be terrifying so a list prepared ahead of time for quick consultation assists in gathering up these essential items with the least amount of stress.

1. **Legal documents**   These include birth certificates, deeds, insurance policies, stock certificates, and other essential paperwork. Discuss

with your accountant and/or attorney about which ones are most important.

2. **Photographs** These cannot be replaced at any cost and are often the most sadly mourned when lost in a house fire. Store negatives at a separate location.
3. **Mementos** Heirlooms, artwork, and other keepsakes.
4. **Jewelry and other valuables** Gold, precious stones, coins, fine art, family silver, antiques, etc.
5. **Family pets**

Arrangements For Animals

Recent fires threatened the Santa Inez Valley, a community of horse ranches that also included valuable cattle and other farm animals. Many of the residents did not have an evacuation plan for their horses, nor did some have access to horse trailers. Most horse trailers will hold only two animals, and when more were present at the homesite, numerous trips were required to ferry them to safety. Often there is not enough time for such luxury.

This illustrates the complications of evacuating animals, particularly when you should be free to defend your house. Animals have survival instincts that cause them to panic at the smell of smoke. Cats and dogs will run and/or hide and may never be found by the time evacuation is ordered. It is best to have secure pet carrying crates for each small animal, and be sure to have them loaded into the car or off site as soon as possible. A recent sad example of what can happen was the Southern California man who went back to his house after the evacuation order to rescue a house cat. The man never returned and was consumed by the flames. No animal is worth your life, or that of any member of your family.

We have all heard tales of large animals such as horses led from a burning barn to safety, then turn and run back "home" into the burning barn. This is a reality, and simply opening the gates to allow the livestock to fend for themselves is not the answer. Trailering large animals, especially when excited and afraid, is no small matter and can be very dangerous. What most people don't consider is where to take the animals, and even more important, who will take care of them once they get there. It is likely you will have to return to the house for other animals or to fight the fire, and without prior arrangements for someone to stable your horses or cattle, you may face a serious dilemma.

If you own livestock, prepare an evacuation plan ahead of time. Even if premature, getting animals out of the area is essential, not only for their safety, but to free you for more important duties. If you don't have a trailer, this allows time to obtain one. Neighbors can be surprisingly generous with their trailers under these conditions, but only after their animals are taken care of. Know exactly where you are going and how long it takes to get there, so if there must be a number of trips you'll allow enough time.

In the Line of Fire—Evacuation Is Imminent

As the fire approaches you may be waiting for the evacuation order. It is wise to evacuate the children and those disabled, ill, or very old before the evacuation is ordered if it looks like the fire is coming toward you. If you are not prepared to defend the house, or lack emergency water supplies, prepare the house and then leave as soon as evacuation is ordered.

There are many things you can do to make the house itself more able to resist ignition and assist fire fighters when they arrive. First of all you must dress for fire because on the front lines there is a perpetual rain of embers or firebrands. They are most apparent when seen at night, glowing bright orange in the dark sky, but appear only as black specks during the day. Some can be very large and cause sizeable burns if they land on your skin. The emphasis on cotton and not synthetic fabrics in the survival packs is because synthetic fibers melt before they burn, and will stick to your skin. No matter how hot the weather, the CDF recommends to dress in long pants and a wool or cotton long-sleeve shirt. The more layers you wear, the less chance of an ember burning through to your skin. Gloves, a dampened bandanna, and non-synthetic hat are also important.

▲▲▲▲▲▲▲▲▲▲▲▲▲▲▲▲▲▲▲▲▲▲▲▲▲▲▲▲▲▲▲▲▲▲▲▲▲▲▲

Coverings for Wall Openings

Frequently overlooked, air vents into attics and crawl spaces become avenues for embers to contact flammable materials indoors. The CDF recommends these openings be covered up with $1/2$-inch or thicker plywood when embers start to fly so they are completely blocked off. You can also cover the outsides of windows with plywood to help insulate them from the heat. Have these panels precut and stored along with a hammer and double-headed foundation nails so they are ready for use. When the fire gets close is not the time to rush around scrounging for material and a saw.

▲▲▲▲▲▲▲▲▲▲▲▲▲▲▲▲▲▲▲▲▲▲▲▲▲▲▲▲▲▲▲▲▲▲▲▲▲▲▲

Load up your getaway car with everything you plan to take with you. Park it in the garage facing out, roll up the windows tightly, and put the keys in the ignition. Close the garage door completely and disconnect the automatic opener so that if the power goes out you can still open the door. Think ahead and plan an evacuation route that will lead away from the path of the fire. To keep abreast of the fire's behavior, keep a portable radio and/or scanner with you at all times. A flashlight is also valuable when the smoke gets thick, or if you are still there at nightfall.

To prepare your house for resisting the fire and assist fire fighters when they arrive, first board up all the vents and windows. The fire fighters must drag hoses and move around quickly, so pull any obstacles such as lawn furniture, barbecues, planters, toys, bicycles, as well as flammable items away from the building.

If you have an emergency water system, make sure it is set up and tested, and a clear path exists so fire trucks can access your reservoir. Where no system is in place, hook up garden hoses to every spigot around the house so they are ready. Set up a sprinkler on your roof, but if you are on a municipal water system don't turn it on until absolutely necessary as this may reduce water pressure somewhere else for fire fighters. Fill all your trash cans and buckets up to the top with water and be sure fire fighters know they are there. Place one or more ladders against the house to assist in accessing the roof.

Once the outside is secure and ready, go indoors and be sure each window and door is completely closed—but not locked. Turn on all the lights. Fill every sink, bathtub, and other large container with water. Shut off any or all natural gas or liquid propane gas (LPG) valves—you should be aware of where each one is well ahead of time. Move flammable window coverings and other household furnishings away from windows. These can be ignited from intense heat radiating through unprotected windows and glass doors. Once all these tasks have been completed, you can leave, or remain behind if there is sufficient water and equipment to douse any ember-generated spot fires around the house.

When the fire is at your door, the heat around the house will be intense. **Don't wait until this point to evacuate because it is already too late.** It is safest to remain inside but do not lock the doors. Keep everyone together and resist going outside. This is a very dangerous emergency situation and ideally everyone should have evacuated by this time. Homeowners with protective firescaping may not experience such intense heat close to the house and are more likely to survive, but firestorm conditions may be overwhelming. If an emergency fire system is operational, remember you have a finite amount of water. Turning it on too soon may cause a shortage later when the fire is much closer. The exact timing is up to you, but it should be operating and make the surrounding surfaces wet before the flames reach the house.

After the Malibu fires this year a couple was found in their charred pickup truck, clearly trying to evacuate, but time had run out. They were attempting to drive down a narrow, vegetation-choked dirt road at the last minute. It's not difficult to imagine what the scene must have been like, and proves how important access is to the defensible homesite. There must have been walls of flame on both sides of the road to create a tunnel of fire. This is why it is recommended you keep the roadway edges cleared of fuel, so that access and evacuation can occur unhindered.

This can happen to anyone who insists on remaining behind beyond the point of reason. If you are trapped as was this couple, try to drive to an open area where fuel volumes are lowest. Stop, close vehicle windows and vents, cover yourself with a blanket or coat and lie on the floor. When evacuating on foot, find a similarly open area and avoid canyons. If you can locate a ditch or swale, lie down flat in the bottom and cover yourself as you would in the car. Ideally a lake, pond, or other open water body not crowded with vegetation would be the safest point.

After the Flames Pass

After the fire has roared through your homesite the danger is not over. If you were fortunate, the house will be still standing but embers may be lodged in nooks and crannies of roofs, siding, and wood decks. Inspect the entire structure closely and douse any hot spots that remain. Climb up into the attic and check for embers there as well. Do not open the windows right away because the fire is sill burning and if the wind shifts it may send ash back in your direction. Walk the property and search for smoking hot spots or burning woodpiles, trees, plants, fences, firewood, outbuildings, and other combustible materials. Look for signs of ground fires that may simply be smouldering in the soil because these can flare up days later. Pay extra close attention to any native trees or shrubs in the outer fire bands. Continue these inspections frequently over the next twelve hours, and keep an eye on any signs of smoke for at least a week.

After the Fire: Erosion Control and Revegetation

The majority of California's damaging wildfires occur during the fire season, which extends from early summer to late fall. The rains here are so unpredictable that the duration of dry fall weather varies considerably from year to year. But in all cases the fire season is ended by the onset of winter rains, and here lies the second great danger.

California's most fire-prone ecosystems occur in foothill and mountain areas. Once these slopes are denuded of vegetation they are highly susceptible to soil erosion, which is proven after nearly every fire by reports of large-scale mud slides. Although the fire may not have touched your homesite, it may still be vulnerable to the effects of erosion in other areas within the same watershed. If the land did burn, whether or not the house was saved, the threat of destabilization of slopes is very real.

Post-fire aerial views of steep hillside subdivisions with every home burned to the ground reveals how tentative the actual foundation area can be. Those homes perched on tiny cut-and-fill pads or split-level footings are vulnerable to total slope failure. These unfortunate residents stand to lose not only the building, but also the actual pads and slopes themselves, which can simply disintegrate under saturation from winter rain. The other aspect to this scenario is that those homes still standing below these burned-out sites are in the path of the mud slides. Add a mild earthquake and the problem increases.

▲▲▲▲▲▲▲▲▲▲▲▲▲▲▲▲▲▲▲▲▲▲▲▲▲▲▲▲▲▲▲▲▲▲▲

Homes such as this one that escaped the flames rest on minute pads. The houses to the right burned to the ground and only a limited footing or pad remains. If serious erosion occurs here, not only will the one remaining house be vulnerable to landslide, what is left of the pads could virtually disappear down the slope.

There are various forms of erosion that relate to how they are controlled, whether by short-term emergency methods, long term stabilization techniques, or both. For Neighbors for Defensible Space on the north shore of Lake Tahoe, erosion is feared for its ability to transport silt from the watersheds around the lake into the crystal clear water. This could be caused by any kind of soil disturbance such as grading, cultivation, logging, or by fires which may expose vast areas of once-forested ground, rendering them vulnerable to soil erosion.

Important Definitions

Erosion	The detachment and transportation of soil particles by the forces of water. (cause)
Sedimentation	The deposit of suspended particles of soil in areas where water movement slows down. (effect)

Imagine how much silt could be dislodged with the runoff from this giant slope. The diversion ditches traversing its surface hardly seem adequate under these conditions.

▲▲

Emergency Assistance

Most people never know the USDA Soil Conservation service exists, but it is a federal government agency that can be of tremendous assistance in soil erosion problems. Through its Emergency Watershed Protection (EWP) program the biologists, engineers, soil scientists, and agronomists work with both citizens and local government to repair the damaged caused by natural disasters such as fire and flood. They offer a tremendous assortment of informative literature for the asking that details erosion control methods, revegetation, and wildlife habitat. Their contributions to the watershed management after many California wildfires has helped reduce subsequent damage from erosion and mudslides which often plague these communities. Homeowners designing firescapes for large-scale projects or those on steeply sloping, erosion-prone sites should consult with the SCS to be sure the proposed erosion control methods are both safe and effective. **Landslides can cause bodily harm and tremendous damage to property. You may be liable if serious conditions are not properly mitigated. For assurance that all factors are addressed, obtain assistance from the SCS or a registered civil engineer.**

▲▲

Soil erosion is not just confined to steep slopes; it can occur on nearly level ground if there is sufficient water movement. If these sites are burned, they too will require some erosion control measures to reduce topsoil losses and prevent siltation into local drainages. The need for an immediate erosion control plan is greater on newly burned steep sites due to the increased potential for large-scale mudslides.

Factors in Choosing Erosion Control Methods

Every drop of rain that falls on bare soil will dislodge a few soil particles, even on an absolutely level site. The degree of slope upon which the particle rests determines whether or not it moves away, and the speed at which it is carried by flowing water. Take a mild slope and add a few hundred thousand raindrops and you have quite a bit of moving soil. This illustrates how erosion control methods must first protect the soil surface from the impact of the raindrop so that the particles remain in place. Second, the controls must slow the movement of the water down the slope so that the particles drop out sooner and are not carried further down.

Under the guidance of federal, state, and county agencies, crews of workers must be at a fire site to shore up burned slopes such as these which become serious hazards after losing their protective covering of vegetation. In this case both highway dividers as well as hundreds of sand bags will help, but not completely resolve the erosion problem.

If you were to study a rock or tree branch on bare ground after a heavy rain you'd notice that on the uphill side there is usually a deposit of fine sand or silt. The rock or branch became an obstacle in the movement of the water, forcing its velocity to slow for a time, and when water slows down the suspended soil particles drop out. Think back to this example when reviewing the erosion-control suggestions in order to better understand how they function on your site.

Finally, the goal of revegetation is to prolong the protection of soil surface particles and bind them into a stronger mass. Plants are the best and least expensive erosion control method we have, but they take time to mature and become most effective. Revegetating with fire-resistant plants will help protect your home from fire when it occurs again—which is more than likely according to most California fire experts.

The Effects of Fire on Soil

Wildfires vary in their intensity and duration. Grass fires burn for a short time and at relatively low temperatures. They can actually increase soil fertility. Fires in dense chaparral and overgrown forests burn much hotter due to the greater proportion of heavy wood fuels such as trees and shrubs. The temperature as well as length of time the fire burns will influence a number of different soil characteristics.

Soils are made up of mineral nutrients, organic matter, and microorganisms all bound together by complex chemical reactions. When superheated by chaparral or forest fires, and continuing for a short while after the fire, organic matter is burned away, nitrogen is consumed, and microorganisms are killed. Many types of grass seed in the upper levels of the soil may also die. The result is considerable decrease in soil fertility, and reduced ability of the area to regenerate quickly from existing seed and thus naturally check surface erosion.

After fires, it is typically the legumes (certain members of the pea family) that are first able to sprout and grow. That's because they obtain nitrogen from the atmosphere, and with special microorganisms in their root systems actually transfer it to the soil. They need not rely on soil nitrogen to survive. Other plants are prevented from thriving as do the legumes because they are starved for nutrients destroyed by the heat.

From this we know soils subjected to chaparral and forest fires must be enriched with organic matter in the form of humus. Typical sources are manure or compost. The soil also benefits from applications of synthetic chemical fertilizers as well to help emergency erosion control grasses get off to a quick start. Since these sites are often on hillsides, fertilizers applied in liquid form help the nutrients to soak directly into the soil and become immediately available. Dry granules require copious amounts of water to dissolve and enter the soil, but the expectant rains will do this job. On gentle slopes and nearly flat land revegetated by seed, granules become a more convenient means of increasing soil nutrient content. For large-scale reforestation, aerial applications of granular fertilizers are used.

Another effect of high heat exposure is a change in soil structure. The heat not only causes deeper soil moisture to evaporate, it also cements soil particles of certain types into very dense layers. Think of this as the difference between ceramic clay and the fired, finished product that is far more cohesive and durable. The hotter the fire (as with a kiln), the more impenetrable the soil becomes. Experts say soil exposure to temperatures of 482° F for only ten minutes is the minimum required to initiate the cementation effect. The earth becomes reluctant or refuses to absorb moisture, which results in increased runoff during the rains. This faster moving water is more likely to dislodge surface particles and cause unwanted erosion and siltation. Moreover, the concrete-like surface presents an inhospitable seedbed for germination of erosion-control plants.

We know the binding effect on soil structure is temporary and will break down, usually within a year. To speed this process the soil may be rototilled or ripped by heavy equipment if not on slopes. Surface scarification with rakes or other hand implements helps seeds to lodge and germinate without risking serious erosion. Mulching of seeds after broadcasting also helps to hold them in place and check surface flow and siltation.

Erosion controls for burn sites are divided into emergency methods and long-term stabilization techniques. In California due to our propensity for mudslides in hillside subdivisions, emergency methods are critical during the first weeks and months following a fire. These protect the surface of the soil as well as reduce siltation. A more long term erosion control plan is based on a permanent firescape band system of landscaping as well as drainage structures, cobblestone riprap, and diversion ditches.

Emergency Erosion Control Measures

These techniques can be divided into two categories, those using man-made materials and those relying on plants. The best choice depends on the degree of slope, soil type, availability of irrigation, cost, and risk of large-scale slope failure. Another factor is the ability to channel runoff away from the slope and thereby reduce the erosion potential.

Plastic Sheeting   Where landslide threat is imminent or when soils on steep slopes are overly saturated, this temporary method separates rain drops from the soil entirely. The plastic must be anchored above the top of the slope so runoff cannot travel underneath the sheet. Attach the top edge per anchor trench diagram. Use only heavy-gauge plastic and stake along all edges to avoid tearing by wind. A disadvantage is that as long as the plastic remains in place it prevents erosion control plants from growing.

Straw Mulch   This is the most widely used immediate erosion control method because it is totally organic, inexpensive, widely available, and easy to transport in neat bale form. A straw mulch not only protects the soil from surface erosion but acts as a filter for sediment. If the slope is to be seeded, broadcast the seed *before* you apply the straw mulch. Distribute the straw in an even layer at least 3 inches thick but loose enough to still see the soil beneath. Estimate approximately 2 tons per acre.

Unless the straw is anchored it will not remain in place for long. If the soil is moist, the straw can be forced or "punched" into the soil, which later hardens as it dries to retain the straw. Small areas can be punched with a shovel by simply pushing the blade down into the earth so many of the straw ends stand upright. Cover the entire slope this way. If the soil is soft enough, just walking back and forth on the straw with stiff boots will suffice.

To further anchor straw mulch upon very steep slopes or those subjected to wind or excessive runoff, lay a secondary covering of matting over the top. You can use jute mesh pegged down securely at regular intervals and around the edges. It will eventually decompose so you need not remove it later on. Other commercial products such as plastic netting, wood excelsior, or even chicken wire will also suffice.

Jute mesh   This widely available netting is made of jute, the organic component in many coarse ropes. To be effective it should be laid upon a seeded slope first covered with a mulch layer of straw, peat, wood shavings, wood chips, or hydromulch. It is sometimes used without the mulch but is much less effective that way. Special U-shaped anchor pins may be purchased to hold the edges and at intervals down the middle of each panel. Secure the top edge with an anchor trench (see diagram). Undyed jute is completely organic in origin and will eventually decompose.

Wood excelsior matting   Similar to jute netting, excelsior matting is more difficult to work with and does not hold up nearly as well as jute. Use only if jute is not available. It may be laid out without

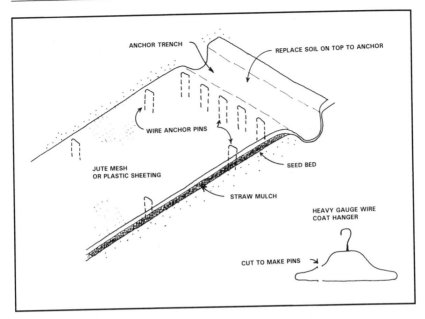

Anchor and Application Diagram for Surface Erosion Control

Jute mesh, plastic, geotextiles, or any other sheet form of erosion control must be securely anchored at the top so it does not creep down the slope with the flow of water. Dig a trench just about a foot deep, and as wide and excavate the soil. Lay the sheeting down in the trench so there is at least 12 inches left over on the upper side of the trench. Then replace the excavated soil on top of the sheeting and tamp it down firmly. You can buy special metal anchor staples or pins, although they can be made in a pinch from heavy gauge wire coat hangers. Note: Although plastic sheeting is shown on this diagram, it should not be used except in emergency where no straw, seed, or jute mesh is applied.

mulch underneath but only if the matting is in multiple layers to 1½ inches thick. If mulch is in place beneath, thickness need be only ½ inch. Excelsior matting is biodegradable and applied as per jute netting instructions above.

Geotextiles There are many new products called geotextiles that have proven to be excellent erosion control materials for difficult slopes. They are woven of space-age fibers and do not readily decompose, thus providing more long term slope stabilization. But like any product they have benefits and problems, such as high cost factors. Before investing in a new geotextile product, consult with a civil engineer or other expert to be sure it is the most effective solution to your erosion control problems.

Straw bale dikes All along the hills of Laguna Canyon, lines of straw bales were placed against the slopes to prevent sedimentation from filling the streets of Laguna Beach. They act like giant brushes filtering sediment out of the moving water and slowing its descent down the canyon walls. Wire-bound bales are valuable as temporary measures in drainage ditches, canyons, swales, and areas where volumes of water and accumulations of silt are expected to be concentrated. The bales are arranged nose-to-tail in a row perpendicular to the expected flow of water. Anchor each end of every bale with a 2x2 wood stake or #3 rebar (concrete reinforcement bar) pounded at least 18 inches into the soil. Dikes are more effective if the bottom portions of bales are buried about 4 inches into the soil. When immediate danger of siltation is past, bales may be taken apart and used as mulch.

In the hollows of this slope long straw-bale siltation dikes have been laid out perpendicular to the flow of water. This not only slows down water velocity, but also captures silt and holds it, so the roadway below is not inundated.

FIRESCAPING TIP

Diversion ditches are very effective small trenches that can channel water away from critical areas. Often water runs across many acres of watershed before it flows down onto a site. Rather than allowing the site to take the brunt of this accumulated runoff, a diversion ditch can be dug across the slope to pick up water and direct it to the side and then down one or both edges of the site. Diversion ditches may be used for both small- and large-scale applications and are simple to dig by hand. Larger concrete-lined diversion ditches can be installed to permanently divert off-site or accumulated runoff around certain areas and are widely used in California's hillside subdivisions.

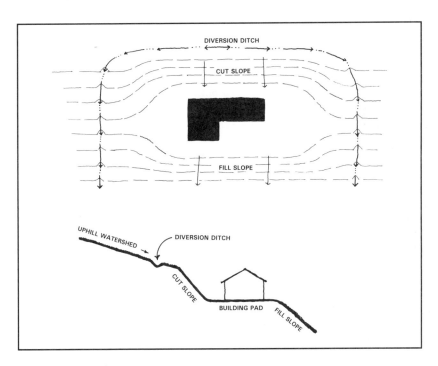

Diversion Ditches

The most common application of diversion ditches is along the top of cut slopes of cut-and-fill building pads.

Seeding for Erosion Control

Seeding burned or newly graded slopes with erosion control grasses and clovers is the most reliable and inexpensive means of stabilizing soil. The down side is that plants take time to germinate, then develop crowns and root systems large enough to hold back surface erosion. But seeding is the only realistic way to deal with the erosion potential of large areas of newly burned soils.

There are many companies that offer their own specialized blend of seed for emergency erosion control, but they all have one species in common: annual ryegrass. Under ideal conditions annual ryegrass germinates in just a few days after sowing, which provides the most immediate plant cover crop possible. Ryegrass is also a cool season grass and will germinate under the lower temperatures of California winters following fire season. Annual rye grows fast and will quickly cover the slope, which buys more time for slower, more deeply rooted perennial grasses such as fescues in the seed mix to become established. **Annual ryegrass is just that, an annual, and should not be considered a permanent solution for erosion control. It is simply the first phase of a more complex erosion control firescaping plan.**

Annual Grasses and Clover Used in Erosion Control Mixes

Bromus mollis	Blando Brome
Lolium multiflorum	Annual Ryegrass
Lolium rigidum	Wimmera-62 Ryegrass
Trifolium hirtum	Hykon Rose Clover
Trifolium subterraneum	Sub Clover
Vulpia myuros	Zorro Annual Fescue

Annual erosion-control seed mixes are made up of plants that germinate quickly from seed, then mature and die off at the end of the season. With regular mowing and irrigation their growing season may be extended slightly but this does not make them perennial. Some varieties may naturally reseed themselves and new plants can sprout each year, but there will be a dormant period beginning when the summer grasses have died back and extending until the winter rains stimulate new seedlings. Therefore, annual erosion control seed mixes are temporary measures.

Perennial Plants In Erosion Control Seed Mixes

Agropyron trichlphorum	Pubescent Wheatgrass
Dactylia glomerata	Orchardgrass

Poa ampla	Sherman Big Bluegrass
Trifolium fragiferum	Strawberry Clover
Trifolium hirtum	Rose Clover
Trifolium repens	Ladino Clover

Erosion-control seed mixes with perennial plants must be irrigated in California to survive year around. Many seed mixes include fast-germinating annuals as well as perennials that remain as permanent erosion control plants after the annuals die out. These include very deep rooting perennial grasses, which send out a vast network of fibrous roots to bind the soil at lower levels. Roots can eventually grow up to three feet deep in some species. Plants develop very large clumps over time, much like the buffalo sod of the midwestern prairie.

Clovers make up a second group of essential erosion-control perennials. These are nitrogen-fixing legumes which will germinate and grow even where nitrogen levels in the soil have been reduced by fire intensity. A bonus of attractive flowers appear if left unmowed, and plants bloom off and on between mowings if well irrigated. Clovers must be watered on a regular basis to live year around in the California climate.

Irrigation

This is an important factor in any erosion control or revegetation plan. If the plants are not irrigated, they must be able to survive on the average rainfall in your area. There are drought-tolerant perennials which

FIRESCAPING TIP

All erosion control seed mixes have a designated application rate expressed as pounds of seed per 1000 square feet or per acre. To order sufficient seed for your project, measure the areas as best you can and then figure how many pounds of seed is required to cover the area. If in doubt, it's better to risk applying too much seed than not enough. Thin or irregular seed distribution may leave areas vulnerable and without sufficient coverage. In general, application rates for erosion-control seed mixes range from .2 to 2.0 pounds per 100 square feet, or from about 5 to 25 pounds per acre. 1 acre = 43,560 square feet.

naturally die back over the summer months, then resprout with the rains. These must be mowed or grazed during the summer to lower fuel volumes created by the dry leaves, seed heads, and resulting chaff. If mowed or cut with a string trimmer, the clippings must be gathered up and removed.

Irrigated sites provide more opportunities for attractive landscapes. Perennial grasses, clovers, herbaceous groundcovers will all remain green year around and many flower profusely. If the plants become too tall, the stand may require a single annual mowing. On steep slopes a string trimmer may be necessary. This is best done in the fall so the winter rains will encourage new lush growth. Creeping shrubs from the fire-resistant lists can also be spotted into this type of landscape.

Planting Erosion Control Seed

There is a time element which influences how erosion control seed mixes are planted on newly burned sites. The goal is to have them firmly in place and well germinated before the heavy rains come. Unirrigated sites ideally should have light rains at first to speed germination so that when heavy rain falls it will not wash out the seed or cause serious erosion. But our fickle California weather can vary so greatly during the fall that hard and fast rules as to planting dates are unreliable. The USDA Soil Conservation Service suggests the period from September 15 to October 15 is timely to seed annuals in the California foothills. This is a bit early in terms of fire revegetation because some of our largest fires have occurred during this time, leaving no choice but to seed the sites much later in winter. This uncertainty is why those who expect serious erosion problems immediately after a fire often resort to mechanical methods such as plastic sheeting, netting, and geotextiles because a planting program is risky.

For smaller sites, broadcasting by hand is the best way to distribute seed, especially if straw or other organic matter and/or netting will be used. Seed remains in place better where the surface of the soil is not smooth but scarred into nooks and crannies where seed may lodge. Seed may be distributed with a belly spreader or lawn fertilizer spreader depending on topography. Remember that seed tends to travel downward with water, so it's a good idea to sow seed more densely at the top of the slope than at the bottom. Once the seed is distributed you can lay out the mulch and netting.

Hydroseeding

For jobs of any size or on inaccessible slopes the *hydroseed* method has

FIRESCAPING TIP

1. Some erosion control seed mixes may include ornamental fountain grass (*Pennisetum setaceum* or *P. ruppelii*). It is added to improve the visual quality of the seeded area but fountain grass is a highly flammable perennial grass and is listed as a species unacceptable for firescaping. Inspect the list of species on a seed mix before you buy to be sure it does *not* include fountain grass.

2. It is a simple matter to incorporate wildflowers into your erosion control mix and some are prepared with the flower seed already included. Where sites are irrigated, seed of other low-growing ornamental flowers can also become part of the revegetation plan. The added color is always welcome on fire-damaged sites or where new grading has disfigured the land. For large-scale projects hire a landscape contractor to help select one of California's fine seed companies to design a specialized mixture for your site. The contractor will know how to set criteria that conforms to your specific irrigation, climate, and soil requirements. This service is too expensive for smaller scale projects, but there are many standard mixes with erosion-control plants, low-growing wildflowers, and even attractive groundcover plants. Here are a few good choices:

   Castilleja chromosa - Indian Paintbrush

   Eschscholzia californica - California Poppy

   Gazania hybrida - Clump Gazania

   Lupinus nanus - Sky Lupine

   Nemophila mensiesii - Baby Blue Eyes

proven highly successful. You may have seen it in use along freeways, where tank trucks spray a solution of fiber, seed, water, and dye onto embankments. This method automatically covers the seed as it is applied and the dye serves to show where and how densely the slurry is sprayed. Dyes are vegetable and soon disappear. Although more expensive than doing the job by hand, hydroseeding can increase germination rates considerably. It also insures far more even coverage, and the fibers help resist seed disturbance from sprinklers or rain.

There is a special organic glue called a *tackifier* which sticks the seed and mulch to very steep slopes where washout is expected. It is mixed into the tank with hydroseed mulch and seed, then sprayed directly upon the slopes. The additional cost of tackifier is a good investment because it helps to discourage seed from rolling down to the bottom of the hill.

Combining Erosion-Control Seed Mixes with Container Plants

In hillside subdivisions throughout Orange County the most successful erosion control plantings on cut-and-fill slopes include both hydroseeding and container-grown plants. Plants can be creeping shrubs from our fire-resistant plant groups, or other species that have a low-growing, minimal fuel volume. The creeping shrubs should be planted first so you won't be walking over the seed or hydroseeding. Plant shrubs and trees in little niches or benches made in the slope. Once these plants are in place, seed can be hydroseeded or broadcast right over the top of them without any damage.

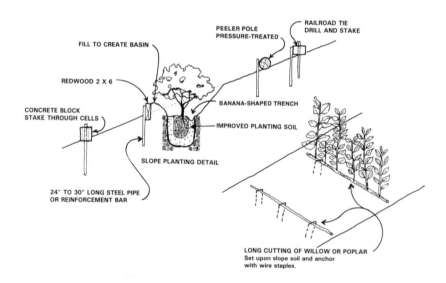

Planting Shrubs and Trees On Slopes

There are many ways to create small pads on slopes where shrubs and trees can be planted. Retaining devices shown here are not absolutely necessary, but they are very helpful in pre venting your pad from eroding. Willow and popular are two types of easy to obtain "wattle" that can be anchored to a slope and will root if given sufficient water. Ideally this should be done in winter while cuttings are leafless, and for greater success these water-loving plants should be well irrigated. Instead of a single cutting, you can bundle up a number of them into a larger barrier that has more immediate effects on reducing runoff velocity and siltation.

Fire-resistant creeping shrubs from lists include

Arctostaphylos spp. - Manzanita

Baccharis spp. - Coyote Bush

Carissa grandiflora 'Green Carpet' - Natal Plum

Ceanothus spp. - California Lilac

Cistus spp. - Rockrose

Lonicera japonica 'Halliana' - Hall's Honeysuckle

Myoporum parvifolium prostrata

Revegetation of Natural Ecosystems with Native Species

In rural parts of California many people own far more land than is required for the firescaping zones. After vast areas of native grasses, chaparral, or forests burn, both the landowners and governmental agencies must face the need for immediate revegetation. If not attended to, our waterways may be seriously affected as silt carried in the winter runoff fills up creeks and rivers to alter wildlife habitat even further.

Revegetation on a large scale is a touchy subject in some ways because there are those who feel only native species should be reintroduced to the wild lands. Many of the grasses and clovers mentioned above are not native, yet they provide the best means of reducing erosion. But when introduced into areas where only native grasses exist, they will quickly take over and virtually crowd out natives. This invasion began in California with the first Spanish livestock two centuries ago, and continues wherever there is grazing.

Many small suppliers of native grass seed are sprouting up all over California because of the demand for wetland preservation and other environmental concerns. Seed and container plants of native shrubs and trees of the chaparral are available as well, but container-grown natives will not take on the same durable characteristics as those grown from seed sown into native soil. You can also gather seed from nearby areas with unburned vegetation to plant on the burned sites. This is particularly valuable because the closer to your site the seed is gathered, the better adapted it will be to your immediate microclimate.

The U.S. Forest Service and the CDF can help you obtain seedling trees grown for reforestation of burned or logged forest lands. These are small, only about 12 inches tall. The bare-root plants, both deciduous and evergreen, are least expensive and available only during the winter months. Container-grown stock can be planted any time of year. There are two sizes available in long, thin containers that look like milk cartons. The larger ones are 40 cubic-inch containers and the smaller measure only 13 cubic inches.

In the resources section of this book is information on the two public nurseries that are closely linked to the CDF. The L. A. Moran Reforestation Center in Davis, California, grows primarily container stock while the Magalia Nursery grows bareroot conifers. These trees are sold to the public for certain uses only, but for other applications contact either of the above nurseries and they will direct you to local private nurseries.

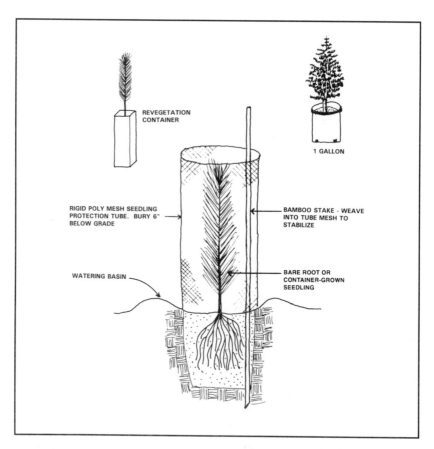

REVEGETATION CONTAINER

1 GALLON

RIGID POLY MESH SEEDLING PROTECTION TUBE. BURY 6" BELOW GRADE

BAMBOO STAKE - WEAVE INTO TUBE MESH TO STABILIZE

WATERING BASIN

BARE ROOT OR CONTAINER-GROWN SEEDLING

Commercially Grown Revegetation Tree Planting Diagram

Whether you plant five seedlings or five hundred, they should all be protected with the mesh protection tube to prevent rabbits and other wildlife from feeding on the succulent little trees. It helps to bury the net into the planting hole a few inches to discourage burrowing animals, but this may prove difficult. The bamboo stakes can be up to 36 inches long and help you know where each tree is located.

Special plastic net sleeves and bamboo anchor stakes can be obtained and will protect each seedling from foraging animals and foot traffic. The plastic sleeve is made of photo-degradable material that eventually decomposes from exposure to sunlight after the seedling matures. The little trees are easy to step on while planting and afterwards if not marked with these devices.

Replanting native oak trees is a simple matter of collecting the acorns and sprouting them. Oaks have long tap roots which help the young plants survive the dryness of their first summer by tapping moisture deep in the soil. This is why they do not grow well in containers and after transplanting the mortality rate is extremely high. Landscape architects and foresters struggled with their oak plantings for years, testing this container and that, various planting seasons and watering, but still the success rate was barely 50 per cent. Those that managed to survive failed to thrive. Studies eventually showed that acorns planted just after they crack open to sprout have an 80- to 90-percent success rate. Today revegetation nurseries grow and sell "cracked" or "sprouted" acorns at certain times of year.

You can either plant acorns or insure their viability by sprouting them before planting. Either way, gather the acorns in the fall and discard any that show discoloration or maggot holes. Then place them in the refrigerator for a month and plant as indicated below. To sprout them first set the acorns in a container of rooting medium such as sand, perlite, or vermiculite and keep moist. Those that are viable will crack slightly within about six weeks and the tip of the root may become visible. That is the time to plant them from 2 to 6 inches deep in native soil. In the chaparral belts acorns lying on *top* of the soil can be found sprouted and the tap root already extending well into the soil. This proves some species of native oaks are not too particular about depth. It helps to use the netting or a stake to mark where each acorn is planted to avoid stepping on them and compacting the soil above the developing stem. Plant extras to allow for natural mortality or losses due to gophers.

To reforest or revegetate extensive areas after burns with native plants, it's a good idea to consult with a professional forester, botanist, or landscape architect before you begin. Their experience and advice will help insure your efforts are successful. Wildlife biologists are also very helpful in reestablishing habitat to encourage regeneration of wildlife in burned areas.

Tips for
Fire-Safe Homesites

Homes are burned down by wildland fires that originate outside the house or a house fire that begins inside. A house fire close to wildlands can ignite a raging forest fire, and every homeowner should realize that there is a perpetual risk of this happening with increasing urban-wildland interface. Should you or your homesite be the source of a wildfire in California, you may be held financially responsible for the costs incurred fighting the blaze and for other damage it causes. Moreover, on May 30, 1991, a new set of fire prevention and loss reduction laws were enacted in California which require defensible space be created and maintained around every homesite. So keeping a fire-safe homesite is now not just an option, but a necessity, as the legal and financial ramifications are awesome indeed.

The CDF publishes some excellent pamphlets detailing all the factors of a fire-safe homesite and house. In this chapter we will look at aspects of a homesite not related to building materials or vegetation. These are covered elsewhere in the book and the assumption is the homesite is defensible in terms of vegetation management. Although often overlooked, these details can lead to serious fires if not attended to, and should be rechecked twice a year.

Fire-safe Maintenance

Power lines   Electrical lines supplying power to a house, or connecting outbuildings often pass through tree canopies, and in some

▲▲

cases are actually attached to trees. Branches rubbing against wires or those close enough to make contact in windy weather are potential hazards. The friction over time will wear down the insulation and ignite the tree. If you see a problem, alert the utility company, since it may be their responsibility to trim back the vegetation. Cut back all tree branches so there are no contacts with the wire, or reroute your wiring so it bypasses the trees. Electrical lines connecting outbuildings that are improperly installed can also be a serious hazard.

Fire wood or scrap lumber   These accumulations of fuel should be stacked at least 30 feet from the house. Most people don't comply because they find it inconvenient to carry their cordwood that far, especially in the snow. If there is a wildfire these fuel stacks become a haven for embers, which will ignite the woodpile, and when in contact with the house, the house is sure to burn as well.

Propane gas tank   Propane tanks are extremely explosive and become a serious threat to fire fighters in any kind of fire. Locate propane tanks no closer than 30 feet from the house for safety. Keep a radius of 10 feet on all sides clear of flammable debris and vegetation.

Access   Be sure fire fighters can find your home quickly. Roads and driveways should be clearly marked and your house address should be displayed with large numbers along with your name if possible. Keep driveways and private roads free of encroaching vegetation and provide turnouts at regular intervals. Get together with your neighbors so their homes are similarly marked to speed response time for any emergency.

Fuel accumulations   Homesites should be kept free of brush piles, accumulations of leaves, garbage, glass, oily rags, and other combustible fuels that may feed a fire. Never use gasoline as a cleaning agent.

Chimney or stove pipe   Sparks rising with smoke from indoor fires is a serious hazard. Cap chimneys and stove pipes with an approved spark arrestor. Keep tree branches pruned at least 15 feet back from the chimney.

Decks   Outdoor wood decking can pose a significant hazard if fuels are allowed to accumulate in the space beneath them. Do not store firewood beneath your deck. Keep all weeds removed with an annual application of herbicide and screen it off or finish with siding.

Safe Rural Burning

In many rural parts of California people burn household and garden refuse outdoors. Wildfires are frequently started by these outdoor bonfires, and the risk of burning should be weighed against other methods of waste disposal. Second, burning of any kind reduces air quality and is not environmentally sound. Despite these drawbacks, there are a few instances when agricultural burning is permissible and perhaps the only way to realistically do away with large accumulations of slash due to land clearing. It is always better to safely burn slash than to leave it piled up indefinitely as a potential fuel pocket for wildfires.

Every county and city in California has its own rules about outdoor debris burning. These can vary considerably so do not use hearsay information. Find out directly from the county yourself! For example, Butte County allows anyone to burn without a permit during the winter until May 1. Humboldt County, on the other hand, not only requires a permit, but restricts burning to designated days. **Always read the entire permit to verify if there are any designated restrictions. Call your local agency that issued the permit before *each* day you intend to burn in order to find out if it is still valid.** Under certain hazardous conditions permits may be rescinded without notice, and it's up to you to find out.

It doesn't take laws or permits to exercise common sense. If you have a permit and insist on burning during improper weather and a wildfire results—you are liable. Permits are not carte blanche to burn indiscriminately. Don't burn on windy days or when it is very hot and dry. Burning when there is a threat of rain during the winter insures any lingering coals will be doused with rainfall. Don't let children, pets, or livestock have access to burning areas. **Do not illegally burn at night to avoid detection.**

There are two ways outdoor burning is usually done. A **burn barrel** is usually an open-topped fifty-gallon drum. It must be fully intact and made of heavy-gauge steel to retain the flames, and tall enough to prevent the material inside from spilling over. It should have a small-mesh (¼ inch minimum) heavy-gauge screen to fit over the top so embers are not allowed to rise up and out of the barrel. There should be at least 10 feet cleared of any combustible materials on all sides of the barrel. Never put aerosol cans, toxic substances, or containers of flammable materials inside a burn barrel. If permits are required, you must have a valid burn permit to incinerate trash in a burn barrel. When the fire burns out, do not dump the ash out in an exposed pile. Dig a hole, pour the ashes into it and wet the mass down, then cover it up again.

Open fires are a popular way to burn garden refuse such as prunings, leaves, tree stumps, and brush. They are piled up over many months or all at once with heavy equipment. One mistake frequently made is trying to burn too large a pile at once, because accumulations of dry chaparral shrubs and trees can fuel an incredibly hot fire. Trying to douse one of these with a garden hose is like spitting into a fireplace. It is better to create a smaller fire near the pile and gradually feed material into it in a controlled fashion. **The fire should be no more than 4 feet in diameter at any time.**

Burn piles should never be placed near forests, buildings, fields, or dry grass. Clear the ground completely before starting to burn and be sure there is at least ten feet cleared on all sides of the fire. A water supply must be close at hand, with a shovel and bucket. Although it is a common practice in rural areas, **do not leave the fire unattended**, even if it is just a smouldering pile of ash. Make sure it is completely extinguished by wetting the ash before you leave.

Poison oak. The characteristic three-leaf pattern of poison oak. It will leaf out bright green in the spring, then develop this reddish tinge in late summer and fall. During winter it is leafless and is difficult to see for most people unless you study the plant and learn the unique qualities of the stems.

FIRESCAPING TIP

If you have had your land cleared by heavy equipment, or are aware of poison oak in a burn pile, be very cautious. Oils from the roots, trunk, branches, leaves, berries, and flowers are all toxic and will travel in the smoke if burned. Poison oak reactions can occur in the mouth, throat, and lungs if the smoke is inhaled, and the eyes may also be affected. If there is a possibility of poison oak in your burn pile, wear a respirator, eye protection, or better yet, don't burn it. For many, contact with burn pile smoke has become a life-threatening experience.

11

Getting Help: Public Agencies and Private Professionals

he majority of this book deals with issues of concern before a wildfire strikes. It is a preventative approach designed to help homeowners in rural areas and those within the urban-wildland interface. Unfortunately, protective measures of establishing defensible space and installation of an emergency water supply are rarely attended to in California. Many readers may now be faced simply with the task of rebuilding a burned-out homesite.

Due to our temperate climate, California benefits from a vast network of agricultural, horticultural, and landscape industry professionals who offer assistance with revegetation or improving fire resistance of homesites. In many cases the services are free of charge, but professionals such as landscape architects and civil engineers are well worth their fees in designing attractive yet highly functional firescapes.

Public Agencies

During these times of tight fiscal constraints within all levels of government, there will be continual changes in the names, scope of work, and services offered by public agencies. Some may disappear altogether. But while they still exist you may take advantage of a wide variety of inexpensive or free literature and benefit from the professionals on staff.

USDA Soil Conservation Service (USCS, SCS)

This federal agency is mentioned numerous times in the text and offers the most valuable of all services. Their offices are scattered throughout California but more commonly in rural areas. Expert in agronomy and civil engineering, their field agents will help to determine soil type, water holding capacity, and vegetation management. They can be of service for the construction of safe and retentive ponds or reservoirs. Large-scale disturbance of vegetation may result in siltation, slope destabilization, and increased runoff somewhere else. This agency helps to identify and mitigate all these potential problems before you begin work.

Their free information sheets detail guidelines for issues concerning soils and plants such as erosion control, wildlife habitat, woodlots, and a variety of other important issues. If the site has recently been burned, contact these offices immediately for an erosion control and revegetation plan. Look for these offices under the federal government listings in your telephone book.

U.S. Fish and Wildlife Service (USFWS)

This is the federal wildlife management agency charged with enforcement of the Endangered Species Act. They are helpful when seeking information regarding wildlife habitat and the future potential for species to be endangered in parts of California which may ultimately influence wildfire vulnerability of existing or proposed homesites. They are also listed under the federal government agencies in your phone book, or can be contacted through the California Department of Fish and Game.

California Department of Fish and Game

Our state agency concerned with wildlife management. It is actively involved in wetland preservation and managing other habitat ecosystems of California. Agents may be willing to make a site visit to assist in any wildlife-related aspects of firescape development and revegetation.

California Department of Forestry and Fire Protection

These experts are in charge of fighting wildfires on both public and private land. They offer a wide assortment of useful fire-prevention literature and an excellent videotape of many of the suggestions detailed in this book. Their agents will make site visits to help point out areas where you may be vulnerable and check on development and maintenance of firescapes. The CDF also has designated Service Foresters who can provide information for both large- and small-scale revegetation projects. Contact the CDF station nearest you for assistance.

CDF State and Region Headquarters

Department Headquarters
1416 Ninth Street
Sacramento, CA 95814
(916) 653–5123

Coastal North Area
135 Ridgeway Avenue,
Santa Rosa, CA 95402
(707) 576–2275

Northern Area Office
6105 Airport Road
Redding, CA 96002
(916) 224–2445

Sierra South Area
1234 East Shaw Avenue
Fresno, CA 93710
(209) 222–3714

Southern Area Office
2524 Mulberry Street
Riverside, CA 92501
(909) 782–4140

Local Fire Station   Many suburban areas are served by municipal fire departments which have experts available to help with fire prevention and development of firescapes. They also offer literature similar to that from the CDF and will make site visits.

University Cooperative Extension Service   There is an excellent network of information and assistance that ties local agriculture to the University of California system. Often labeled "Farm Advisor" they may be found listed in your county government section of the phone book. They offer either free or very low cost booklets and information sheets on a variety of topics from landscaping to farming. Agents may be willing to make a site visit for serious issues such as plant diseases in firescapes.

University of California Agricultural Publications

Send or call for free catalog to

Publications
University of California
Agriculture and Natural Resources
6701 San Pablo Avenue
Oakland, CA 94608-1239
(415) 642–2431

City or County Public Works or Planning Departments
In many parts of the state there are strict codes as to what is allowable

in terms of vegetation management on a piece of property. Some private communities require permission from homeowner's associations to remove trees or even native shrubs. It is important to discuss with your local planning department any large-scale vegetation adjustments for firescapes. This goes for reservoir and pond construction as well.

Private Professionals

Private-sector experts can be hired for an hourly fee to design a firescape and emergency water system. They are not usually bound by the limitations of government employees and as long as you are willing to pay the fees, they will continue to work on your project. It's important to know that in recent years there has been a dramatic rise in fee schedules for these professionals due to more stringent licensing requirements and the costs of litigation. You can expect to pay from $50 to $150 per hour for any one of them.

These fees are for *licensed* professionals, and each will have a registration number with the California Department of Consumer Affairs in Sacramento. There are many unlicensed people who are quite knowledgeable but you have no means of knowing whether or not they are qualified for the task. To protect yourself from liability, hire only a licensed professional so there is no question as to who is responsible if there is a problem. To verify if an individual is licensed, contact the State of California Department of Consumer Affairs to inquire if the license is indeed active and whether there have been any complaints filed.

Architect   A licensed architect will be informed as to the fire resistance of various building materials and should also be able to design a home with cutting-edge fireproof qualities. An architect can also help you replace certain features of an existing home to make it less vulnerable to fire.

Landscape Architect   A landscape architect is the best person to help you with firescaping, but inquire whether or not he or she has experience in this field. These professionals will help you to combine fire-resistant plants along with other materials into an attractive landscape. Landscape architects must also by licensed by the state.

Civil Engineer   For design of emergency water supply and a delivery system, a licensed civil engineer is the best choice for calculating the proper fire water flows. Often an older, partially retired engineer who retains a valid license can be more economically hired to develop systems than a full-time engineer with a busy practice. Because the water storage and delivery can be expensive to install and must function perfectly, it is best to have it professionally designed to avoid any problems down the road. Engineers are also invaluable in issues of slope stabilization, and design of retaining walls and extensive drainage devices.

Landscape Contractor   If you aren't going to plant your own firescape, a licensed landscape contractor may be able to design an attractive planting plan using plants detailed in this book. There should be a plan prepared ahead of time showing how the planting will look, then an installation cost prepared. This professional can also design and install an irrigation system for the firescape as well. Verify this license by calling the Department of Consumer Affairs.

Forester or Registered Arborist   These are experts who deal exclusively in trees and should be consulted before any large-scale tree removal is done. They can help evaluate the health of every tree and provide guidance as to which individuals or species should be either preserved or removed. Other factors such as longevity, wind loading, and structural form will influence the safest, most successful forest and tree management. Foresters can assist if selective logging is required to thin out overcrowded forests on larger scale properties. These professionals should be members of either the American Forestry Association, American Society of Consulting Arborists, International Society of Arboriculture, or the National Arborist Association.

Tree Service   The tree service industry is not well regulated and you can be vulnerable to unscrupulous operators or considerable liability if something goes wrong. Ask for references, proof of insurance, and contractor's license, and verify all of these before hiring. Those companies owned by arborists or foresters are more likely to do a sensitive job. For large jobs, consult a second company for a comparative estimate just as you would seek more than one medical opinion before submitting to surgery. Be sure to discuss costs of clean up and hauling.

Emotional Support

For those who have experienced a wildfire first hand, the faintest whiff of smoke in the air will kindle instant panic. People who have lost their homes may never overcome the fear of fire. Others who may not be close to fires but see the devastation on the evening news may grow just as paranoid as the actual victims. Fear of wildfires is nothing to scoff at and should be treated as other overwhelming phobias by a trained professional. If left untreated the fear may grow to unmanageable proportions and become difficult to live with.

Mental health professionals tell us that those who have lost a home to fire feel the same kind of grieving as they would for a dead loved one. The memories, possessions, household pets, even the sense of self can be destroyed with one's place of residence. To rebuild may seem an insurmountable task even if there are sufficient funds from insurance.

Unlike an isolated house fire, whole communities can be devastated by wildfires, which leaves many with nowhere to live, and no place to go home to. While flood waters recede, burned-out neighborhoods perish entirely. It is likely there will be mental health professionals available to fire victims and therapy groups organized. Contact local mental health organizations for news on new groups.

The trauma of wildfire may also be eased by a private counselor or psychiatrist. These professionals can assist over the long term with easing the losses and the fear of reoccurring fires. Many HMOs will cover part or all the costs of this type of counseling.

▲▲▲▲▲▲▲▲▲▲▲▲▲▲▲▲▲▲▲▲▲▲▲▲▲▲▲▲▲▲▲▲▲▲▲▲▲▲▲

RESOURCES

Obtaining Plants

All of the plants listed in this book are widely available throughout California and best purchased from a full-service nursery or garden center. We are fortunate to have such a vast nursery industry here on the West Coast, and most retail plant sellers have broad access to even the most obscure species. These sources may not always have what you need in stock, especially when it comes to iceplant, but they have access to these plants from wholesale growers and will special order them for you.

When professional landscapers prepare for a sizeable job, they order all the plants ahead of time from the nursery. This allows for the retailer to assemble the entire order in one place when supplied by a number of different wholesale growers. Although you may not be planting an entire landscape at once, the need to pre-order is still important. This provides fresh plants of the proper variety in containers best suited to your project.

The listings below are mail-order sources that will ship their products anywhere in California and in some cases neighboring states. If your local nursery is having difficulty finding the plants you are looking for, contact the California Association of Nurserymen. Members are qualified growers, with many specializing in the subjects that follow. Although many are wholesale, they may still serve the retail trade, or will gladly sell to your local nursery or landscape contractor.

California Association of Nurserymen
4620 Northgate Boulevard Suite 155
Sacramento, CA 95834
(916) 567–0200

▲▲▲▲▲▲▲▲▲▲▲▲▲▲▲▲▲▲▲▲▲▲▲▲▲▲▲▲▲▲▲▲▲▲▲▲▲▲

Seed Sources for Erosion Control
and Irrigated Pasture

Bulk seed for revegetation and erosion control is widely available throughout California at agricultural suppliers, feed stores, and retail nurseries. Buying directly from a local supplier will save you shipping charges, particularly for large, heavy orders. Wildflowers are sold either as individual species or predesigned mixes. These are the best places to find a wide variety to choose from, and seed is more economically priced in bulk, by the pound.

Applewood Seed Co.
5380 Vivial Street
Arvada, CO 80002
(303) 431–6283

Color catalog of bulk wildflower and clumping meadow grasses. Good source of low-fuel-volume mixes: Knee-Hi mixture, Low Growing mixture, Super-short Mixture. Grasses: buffalo grass, fescues.

Clyde Robin Seed Company
P.O. Box 2366
Hayward, CA 94546
(415) 785–0425
Free color catalog

Well-illustrated catalog of wildflowers and specialized mixes. Low-growing mowable mixes for minimal fuel volumes. Mowable species.

Moon Mountain Wildflowers
P.O. Box 34
Morro Bay, CA 93442
(805) 772–2473
Catalog $2.00

Catalog of bulk wildflower seed. Erosion-control mix, grassland wildflower mix, drought-tolerant mix, California native mix. Specialized California mixes for coast, central valley, mountain, all perennial, and urban mix.

Peaceful Valley Farm Supply
P.O. Box 2209
Grass Valley, CA 95945
(916) 272–4769
B/W Catalog $2.00

Extensive 100-page catalog. Supplies: jute netting.

Bulk seed: erosion-control seed mix, dryland erosion and cover mix, quick-cover erosion mix, various wildflower seed mixes, cover crop legume seed mixes, wide variety of clovers and clover mixes. Also dryland range and irrigated pasture seed mixes. Custom seed mixes available. Quantity discounts.

Pecoff Bros. Nursery & Seed, Inc.
Route 5, Box 215R
Escondido, Ca 92025
(619) 744–3120
No catalog.

Strictly a large-scale grower specializing in serious erosion control problems, saline soils, and extreme drought. Excellent resource for community-level erosion control and revegetation projects. Seed mix design service and on-site consultation available.

Plants of the Southwest
Agua Fria, Route 6, Box 11A
Santa Fe, NM 87505
(800) 788–7333
Color catolog $3.50

Great source of plants and seed for dry land gardens. Drought-tolerant grasses.

Tree Farms for Native Revegetation

There are dozens of wholesale tree farms throughout California, but only a few are open to the public. It's best to inquire at your local CDF station or ask a retail nursery for the best sources in your area. A professional forester or registered arborist can also direct you to reliable local growers. Revegetation seedlings are grown differently than standard landscape trees because for reforestation thousands of seedlings may be planted in a single season over a very large area. Therefore they are either supplied in compartmentalized styrofoam blocks, thin tubes, or bare root. This is the rare situation where conifer trees are sold bare root.

Forest Farm
990 Tetherow Road
Williams, Oregon 97544-9599
(503) 846–7269
Catalog $3.00 (not illustrated but extensive)

Grower of wide variety of trees, shrubs, and perennials in planting tubes, the preferred form for rapid planting on large-scale projects. Native and introduced species.

Revegetation Poplars

Geo. Zappettini Co.
17844 Yosemite Road
Tuolumne, CA 95379
(209) 928–3468

George Zappettini is a retired forester and produces some of the most versatile and vigorous trees for a variety of purposes. His poplars are a "cottonless" version of western cottonwood, and after many years of hunting he has found what is considered the perfect tree. May be the fastest-growing tree available; fibrous roots bind soils, it is nontoxic to people or animals, and inexpensive to buy. He sells only bare-root poles of different sizes that ship easily, but only from December 1 to March 31 each year. Reserve your stock ahead of time.

California Department of Forestry Tree Farms

These two suppliers are geared to large-scale revegetation and supply trees for use in reforestation, erosion control, windbreaks, Christmas trees, and fuel wood. Revegetation of recently burned land falls within the usage limitations. The seedlings are not to be used for landscaping, resale, or distribution in other ways. Minimum order is one hundred seedling trees. Call or write for free availability list and current pricing. They will also send a list of CDF forest advisors for each California county as well as detailed information on selection of native tree species for revegetation and proper planting instructions.

Megalia Nursery
6640 Steiffer Road
Megalia, CA 95954
(916) 873–0400

Major supplier of seedling evergreen bare-root tree stock. Other species of native trees and shrubs. Provides government agencies with native trees for reforestation of burned or logged land.

L. A. Moran Reforestation Center
5800 Chiles Road
P.O. Box 1590
Davis, CA 95617
(916) 322–2299

Supplier of container seedling forest trees. Oaks and other species of native trees and shrubs.

Drought- and Frost-Tolerant Cacti and Succulents

Henrietta's Nursery
1345 North Brawley
Fresno, CA 93722-5899
(209) 275–2166
B/W catalog $1.00

Broad source for both drought- and cold-tolerant cacti and succulents.

A High Country Garden
2902 Rufina Street
Santa Fe, NM 87501-2929
(505) 438–3031

Free color catalog with frost tolerant cacti and succulents.

Water Tanks

Water tanks can be constructed out of wood, metal, fiberglass, and plastic. The majority of water tanks sold in California are plastic, which hold up well and are more lightweight for shipping. Some feed stores or farm supply houses keep a few plastic tanks on hand or they will order one for you. You will also find listings in the yellow pages of your telephone book under the heading of "Tanks."

A premier supplier of plastic and galvanized steel water tanks is California Tank Distributors. They are knowledgeable regarding the water storage requirements of many communities that require a fire reservoir. They ship virtually anywhere and pick up the freight charges so all you pay for is the tank. The owner, Peter Reimuller, guarantees every product and is available to assist you with selection of the right tank for your location and specific needs. Hydrants for the tanks are also available. Free catalog and price list.

California Tank Distributors
P.O. Box 3
Point Arena, CA 95468
(800) 655–9100
FAX (707) 882–2488

▲▲

Very High Fire Hazard Severity Zones Law
Assembly Bill No. 337
(The Bates Bill)

Note: For more information on this act, contact the California
Department of Forestry or your local firefighting agency.

An act to add Chapter 6.8 (commencing with Section 51175) to Part 1 of
Division 1 of Title 5 of the Government Code, and to amend Section 13108.5
of the Health and Safety Code, relating to fire protection.

LEGISLATIVE COUNSEL'S DIGEST

AB 337, Bates. Very high fire hazard severity zones.
(1) Under existing law, the State Board of Forestry is required to classify
all lands within the state, in accordance with prescribed criteria, for the purpose of determining areas in which the financial responsibility of preventing
and suppressing fires is primarily the responsibility of the state.
This bill would declare that the prevention of fires is not a municipal
affair but is instead, a matter of statewide concern, and would make a finding
and declaration of the Legislature that its provisions apply to all local agencies, including, but not limited to, charter cities, charter counties, and charter
cities and counties. The bill would prohibit that finding from limiting the
authority of a local agency, as defined, from imposing more restrictive fire
and panic safety requirements, as otherwise authorized by law.
The bill would state that it is not the intent of the Legislature to limit or
restrict the authority of a local agency to impose more restrictive fire and
panic safety requirements, as otherwise authorized by law.
This bill would require the Director of Forestry and Fire Protection to
identify areas in the state as very high fire hazard severity zones within all
counties pursuant to a prescribed schedule. The bill would require local agencies, as defined, to designate, by ordinance, very high fire hazard severity
zones in their jurisdiction after receiving recommendations from the director,
except as prescribed. The bill would authorize local agencies to include or
exclude areas following certain findings and would require changes made by
local agencies to be final and not rebuttable by the director. By requiring local
agencies to designate very high fire hazard severity zones within their jurisdictions, this bill would impose a state-mandated local program. The bill
would require the State Fire Marshal to prepare and adopt a model ordinance
that provides for the establishment of any high fire hazard security zones.
(2) Under existing law, any person who owns, leases, controls, operates,
or maintains any building or structure in, upon, or adjoining any mountainous area or forest-covered lands, brush-covered lands, or grass-covered

▲▲

lands, or any land that is covered with flammable material, is required to undertake specific fire protection measures, including the maintenance of specified firebreaks.

The bill would enact requirements of this nature for any person who owns, leases, controls, operates, or maintains, any occupied dwelling or occupied structure in, upon, or adjoining any mountainous area, forest-covered land, brush-covered land, grass-covered land, or land covered with flammable material, which area or land is within a very high fire hazard severity zone, as described in (1).

The bill would authorize local agencies to exempt certain structures and would exempt certain land or water areas.

The bill would make violation of these requirements an infraction or misdemeanor, as specified, thereby imposing a state-mandated local program by creating a new crime, and would specify related matters.

This bill would require local agencies to notify owners of property of violation and would authorize local agencies to correct the conditions and make a lien upon the property, as prescribed. By creating these requirements, this bill would impose a state-mandated local program.

The bill would permit a violation of these requirements to be considered a public nuisance, as specified.

(3) Existing law requires the State Fire Marshal to adopt, amend, and repeal regulations for roof coverings and openings into the attic areas of buildings in those fire hazard severity zones in state responsibility lands as designated by the director. Existing law requires the director to classify lands within state responsibility areas into fire hazard severity zones.

This bill would instead require the State Fire Marshal to propose, and would require the State Building Standards Commission to adopt, amend, and repeal those regulations. The bill would also require the State Fire Marshal to propose, and would require the State Building Standards Commission to adopt, amend, and repeal, those regulations for buildings in very high fire hazard severity zones in state responsibility lands, designated by the director, and in very high fire hazard severity zones as described in (1). The bill would require roofs on all new buildings and certain existing buildings in both of those zones to be at least a class B roof that complies with Standard 32-7 of the Uniform Building Code, as adopted in the California Building Standards Code. The bill would impose requirements on installers and roofing materials and make other related changes. The bill would exempt historic buildings, as defined, from these provisions.

(4) The bill would require its provisions to prevail in the case of conflict with certain other state law and in the case of certain other bills being chaptered into law.

(5) The California Constitution requires the state to reimburse local agencies and school districts for certain costs mandated by the state. Statutory provisions establish procedures for making that reimbursement.

This bill would provide that no reimbursement is required by this act for specified reasons.

However, this bill would provide that, if the Commission on State Mandates determines that this bill contains other costs mandated by the state, reimbursement for those costs shall be made pursuant to those statutory procedures and, if the statewide cost does not exceed $1,000,000, shall be made from the State Mandates Claims Fund.

The people of the State of California do enact as follows:

SECTION 1. Chapter 6.8 (commencing with Section 51175) is added to Part 1 of Division 1 of Title 5 of the Government Code, to read:

CHAPTER 6.8 VERY HIGH FIRE HAZARD SEVERITY ZONES

51175. The Legislature hereby finds and declares as follows:

(a) Fires are extremely costly, not only to property owners and residents, but also to local agencies. Fires pose a serious threat to the preservation of the public peace, health, or safety. Since fires ignore civil boundaries, it is necessary that cities, counties, special districts, state agencies, and federal agencies work together to bring raging fires under control. Preventive measures are therefore needed to ensure the preservation of the public peace, health, or safety.

(b) The prevention of fires is not a municipal affair, as that term is used in Section 5 of Article XI of the California Constitution, but is instead, a matter of statewide concern. It is the intent of the Legislature that this chapter apply to all local agencies, including, but not limited to, charter cities, charter counties, and charter cities and counties. This subdivision shall not limit the authority of a local agency to impose more restrictive fire and panic safety requirements, as otherwise authorized by law.

(c) It is not the intent of the Legislature in enacting this chapter to limit or restrict the authority of a local agency to impose more restrictive fire and panic safety requirements, as otherwise authorized by law.

51176. The purpose of this chapter is to classify lands in the state in accordance with whether a very high fire hazard is present so that public officials are able to identify measures that will retard the rate of spread, and reduce the potential intensity, of uncontrolled fires that threaten to destroy resources, life, or property, and to require that those measures be taken.

51177. As used in this chapter:

(a) "Director" means the Director of Forestry and Fire Protection.

(b) "Very high fire hazard severity zone" means an area designated by the director pursuant to Section 51178 that is not a state responsibility area.

(c) "Local agency" means a city, county, city and county, or district responsible for fire protection within a very high fire hazard severity zone.

(d) "Single specimen tree" means any live tree that stands alone in the landscape so as to be clear of buildings, structures, combustible vegetation, or other trees, and that does not form a means of rapidly transmitting fire from the native growth to any occupied dwelling or structure.

(e) "State responsibility areas" means those areas identified pursuant to Section 4102 of the Public Resources Code.

51178. (a) The director shall identify areas in the state as very high fire hazard severity zones based on consistent statewide criteria and based on the severity of fire hazard that is expected to prevail in those areas. Very high fire hazard severity zones shall be based on fuel loading, slope, fire weather, and other relevant factors.

(b) On or before January 1, 1995, the director shall identify areas as very high fire hazard severity zones in the Counties of Alameda, Contra Costa, Los Angeles, Marin, Napa, Orange, Riverside, San Bernardino, San Francisco, San Mateo, Santa Barbara, Santa Clara, Solano, Sonoma, and Ventura. This information shall be transmitted to all local agencies with identified very high fire hazard severity zones within 30 days.

(c) On or before January 1, 1996, the director shall identify areas as very high fire hazard severity zones in all other counties. This information shall be transmitted to all local agencies with identified high fire hazard severity zones within 30 days.

51179.   (a) A local agency shall designate, by ordinance, very high fire hazard severity zones in its jurisdiction within 120 days of receiving recommendations from the director pursuant to subdivisions (b) and (c) of Section 51178. A local agency shall be exempt from this requirement if ordinances of the local agency, adopted on or before December 31, 1992, impose standards that are equivalent to, or more restrictive than, the standards imposed by this chapter.

(b) A local agency may, at its discretion, exclude from the requirements of Section 51182 an area identified as a very high fire hazard severity zone by the director within the jurisdiction of the local agency, following a finding supported by substantial evidence in the record that the requirements of Section 51182 are not necessary for effective fire protection within the area.

(c) A local agency may, at its discretion, include areas within the jurisdiction of the local agency, not identified as very high fire hazard severity zones by the director, as very high fire hazard severity zones following a finding supported by substantial evidence in the record that the requirements of Section 51182 are necessary for effective fire protection within the area.

(d) Changes made by a local agency to the recommendations made by the director shall be final and shall not be rebuttable by the director.

(e) The State Fire Marshal shall prepare and adopt a model ordinance that provides for the establishment of very high fire hazard severity zones.

(f) Any ordinance adopted by a local agency pursuant to this section that substantially conforms to the model ordinance of the State Fire Marshal shall be presumed to be in compliance with the requirements of this section.

51180.   For the purposes of Division 3.6 (commencing with Section 810) of Title 1, vegetation removal or management, undertaken in whole or in part, for fire prevention or suppression purposes shall not be deemed to alter the natural condition of public property. This section shall apply only to natural conditions of public property and shall not limit any liability or immunity that may otherwise exist pursuant to this chapter.

51181.   The director shall periodically review the areas in the state identified as very high fire hazard severity zones pursuant to this chapter, and as necessary, shall make recommendations relative to very high fire hazard severity zones. This review shall coincide with the review of state responsibility area lands every five years and, when possible, fall within the time frames for each county's general plan update. Any revision of areas included in a very high fire hazard severity zone shall be made in accordance with Sections 51178 and 51179.

51182. (a) Any person who owns, leases, controls, operates, or maintains any occupied dwelling or occupied structure in, upon, or adjoining any mountainous area, forest-covered land, brush-covered land, grass-covered land, or any land that is covered with flammable material, which area or land is within a very high fire hazard severity zone designated by the local agency pursuant to Section 51179, shall at all times do all of the following:

(1) Maintain around and adjacent to the dwelling or structure a firebreak made by removing and clearing away, for a distance of not less than 30 feet on each side thereof or to the property line, whichever is nearer, all flammable vegetation or other combustible growth. This paragraph does not apply to single specimens of trees, ornamental shrubbery, or similar plants that are used as ground cover, if they do not form a means of rapidly transmitting fire from the native growth to any dwelling or structure.

(2) Maintain around and adjacent to the occupied dwelling or occupied structure additional fire protection or firebreaks made by removing all brush, flammable vegetation, or combustible growth that is located from 30 feet to 100 feet from the occupied dwelling or occupied structure or to the property line, whichever is nearer, as may be required by the local agency if the local agency finds that, because of extra hazardous conditions, a firebreak of only 30 feet around the occupied dwelling or occupied structure is not sufficient to provide reasonable fire safety. Grass and other vegetation located more than 30 feet from the dwelling or structure and less than 18 inches in height above the ground may be maintained where necessary to stabilize the soil and prevent erosion.

(3) Remove that portion of any tree that extends within 10 feet of the outlet of any chimney or stovepipe.

(4) Maintain any tree adjacent to or overhanging any building free of dead or dying wood.

(5) Maintain the roof of any structure free of leaves, needles, or other dead vegetative growth.

(6) Provide and maintain at all times a screen over the outlet of every chimney or stovepipe that is attached to any fireplace, stove, or other device that burns any solid or liquid fuel. The screen shall be constructed and installed in accordance with the California Building Standards Code.

(b) A person is not required under this section to maintain any clearing on any land if that person does not have the legal right to maintain the clearing, nor is any person required to enter upon or to damage property that is owned by any other person without the consent of the owner of the property.

51183. (a) The local agency may exempt from the standards set forth in Section 51182 structures with exteriors constructed entirely of nonflammable materials, or conditioned upon the contents and composition of the structure, and may vary the requirements respecting the removing or clearing away of flammable vegetation or other combustible growth with respect to the area surrounding the structures. In no case shall this subdivision be deemed to authorize a local agency to vary any requirement that is a building standard subject to Section 18930 of the Health and Safety Code, except as otherwise authorized by law.

(b) No exemption or variance shall apply unless and until the occupant thereof, or if there be no occupant, then the owner thereof, files with the local agency a written consent to the inspection of the interior and contents of the structure to ascertain whether the provisions of Section 51182 are complied with at all times.

51184.   (1) Section 51182 shall not apply to any land or water area acquired or managed for one or more of the following purposes or uses:

(1) Habitat for endangered or threatened species, or any species that is a candidate for listing as an endangered or threatened species by the state or federal government.

(2) Lands kept in a predominantly natural state as habitat for wildlife, plant, or animal communities.

(3) Open space lands that are environmentally sensitive parklands.

(4) Other lands having scenic values, as declared by the local agency, or by state or federal law.

(b) This exemption applies whether the land or water area is held in fee title or any lesser interest. This exemption applies to any public agency, any private entity that has dedicated the land or water areas to one or more of those purposes or uses, or any combination of public agencies and private entities making that dedication.

(c) This section shall not be construed to prohibit the use of properly authorized prescribed burning to improve the biological function of land or to assist in the restoration of desired vegetation.

(d) In the event that any lands adjacent to any land or water area described in subdivision (a) are improved such that they are subject to Section 51182, the obligation to comply with Section 51182 shall be with the person owning, leasing, controlling, operating or maintaining the occupied dwelling or occupied structure on the improved lands. All maintenance activities and other fire prevention measures required by Section 51182 shall be required not only for the improved lands, not the land and water areas described in subdivision (a).

51185.   (a) A violation of Section 51182 is an infraction punishable by a fine of not less than one hundred dollars ($100) nor more than five hundred dollars ($500).

(b) If a person is convicted of a second violation of Section 51182 within five years, that person shall be punished by a fine of not less than two hundred fifty dollars ($250) nor more than five hundred dollars ($500).

(c) If a person is convicted of a third violation of Section 51182 within five years, that person is guilty of a misdemeanor and shall be punished by a fine of not less than five hundred dollars ($500).

51186.   The local agency having jurisdiction of property upon which conditions regulated by Section 51182 are being violated shall notify the owner of the property to correct the conditions. If the owner fails to correct the conditions, the local agency may cause the corrections to be made, and the expenses incurred shall become a lien on the property that is the subject of the corrections when recorded in the county recorder's office in the county in which the real property is located. The priority of the lien shall be as of the date of recording. The lien shall contain the legal description of the real property, the assessor's parcel number, and the name of the owner of record as shown on the latest equalized assessment roll.

51187.   Any violation of Section 51182 may be considered a public nuisance pursuant to Section 38773.

51188.   In the instance of conflict between this chapter and any provision of state law that allows a regional planning agency to regulate very high fire hazard severity zones, this chapter shall prevail.

SEC. 2.   Section 13108.5 of the Health and Safety Code is amended to read:

13108.5.   (a) The State Fire Marshal shall propose, and the State Building Standards Commission shall adopt, amend, and repeal regulations for roof coverings and openings into the attic areas of buildings in those fire hazard severity zones designated by the Director of Forestry and Fire Protection pursuant to Article 9 (commencing with Section 4201) of Chapter 1 of Part 2 of Division 4 of the Public Resources Code.

(b) The State Fire Marshal shall, on or before July 1, 1993, propose, and the State Building Standards Commission shall adopt, amend, and repeal regulations for roof coverings and openings into the attic areas of buildings in very high fire hazard severity zones designated by the Director of Forestry and Fire Protection pursuant to Article 9 (commencing with Section 4201) of Chapter 1 of Part 2 of Division 4 of the Public Resources Code and in very high fire hazard severity zones designated by a local agency pursuant to Chapter 6.8 (commencing with Section 51175) of Part 1 of Division 1 of Title 5 of the Government Code. Roofs on all buildings in both of those very high fire hazard severity zones shall be at least a class B roof that complies with Standard 32-7 of the Uniform Building Code, as adopted in the California Building Standards Code.

(c) This section shall apply to new buildings and to existing buildings when 50 percent or more of the roof area is reroofed within a one-year period after the issuance of a building permit. When there is no building permit issued this section is applicable to buildings constructed after January 1, 1993, and to buildings where 50 percent or more of the roof area is reroofed within a one-year period after commencing construction.

(d) The installer of the roof covering shall provide certification of the roof covering classification to the building owner, and when requested, to the inspection authority having jurisdiction. The installer shall also install the roof covering in accordance with the manufacturer's listing.

(e) The roofing material shall have passed a minimum 10 year accelerated weather test approved by a testing laboratory recognized by the State Fire Marshal.

(f) A city, county, or city and county may impose more restrictive requirements than those imposed by this section under the authority of Sections 13143.2 and 13143.5. Nothing in this section shall limit the authority of a city, county, city and county, or special district to impose more restrictive requirements than those imposed by this section, for areas that are not identified as very high fire hazard severity zones.

(g) The regulations proposed by the State Fire Marshal and adopted by the State Building Standards Commission pursuant to subdivision (a) shall be consistent with the rules and regulations adopted pursuant to Section 17922. The regulations shall be enforced by the agency responsible for enforcement of this part within each zone.

(h) This section shall not apply to any building or facility designated as an historic building, as defined in Section 18955.

SEC. 3. If AB 2131 or SB 1321, or both, are chaptered during the 1991–92 Regular Session and require, upon a specified date, at least a class C rated roof covering under specified conditions in all jurisdictions within the state, and this bill is chaptered during the 1991–92 Regular Session and requires a class B roof covering in specific zones or areas in accordance with specified conditions, this bill shall apply to structures located within areas designated by a local agency as very high fire hazard severity zones pursuant to Chapter 6.8 (commencing with Section 51175) of Part 1 of Division 1 of Title 5 of the Government Code, and areas designated by the Director of Forestry and Fire Protection as very high fire hazard severity zones pursuant to Article 9 (commencing with Section 4201) of Chapter 1 of Part 2 of Division 4 of the Public Resources Code, and at least the class C rated roof covering shall apply elsewhere in the state.

SEC. 4. No reimbursement is required by this act pursuant to Section 6 of Article XIII B of the California Constitution as a result of costs which may be incurred by a local agency or school district because this act creates a new crime or infraction, changes the definition of a crime or infraction, changes the penalty for a crime or infraction, or eliminates a crime or infraction.

In addition, no reimbursement is required by this act pursuant to Section 6 of Article XIII B of the California Constitution because the Legislature finds and declares that, for certain costs imposed by this act, there are savings as well as costs in this act which, in the aggregate, do not result in additional net costs.

However, notwithstanding Section 17610 of the Government Code, if the Commission on State Mandates determines that this act contains other costs mandated by the state, reimbursement to local agencies and school districts for those costs shall be made pursuant to Part 7 (commencing with Section 17500) of Division 4 of Title 2 of the Government Code. If the statewide cost of the claim for reimbursement does not exceed one million dollars ($1,000,000), reimbursement shall be made from the State Mandates Claims Fund. Notwithstanding Section 17580 of the Government Code, unless otherwise specified in this act, the provisions of this act shall become operative on the same date that the act takes effect pursuant to the California Constitution.

▲▲

Index

▲▲

Sedum confusum, 77
Serbian bellflower (*Campanula poscharskyana*), 91
Shrub canopy, 62
Shrubs, 70–72, 84–89, 130
  spacing of, 61, 64
Siding, 29
Silver spreader (*Artemisia caucasica*), 78
Snow in summer (*Cerastium tomentosum*), 80
Soil
  fire's effect on, 120–21
  moisture, 39
Spreading plants, 71, 72
Spring cinquefoil (*Potentilla verna*), 81
Squaw carpet (*Ceanothus prostratus*), 86
Sunrose (*Helianthemum nummularium*), 86
Survival pack, 107–109
Swimming pools, 45
Sycamore (*Platanus racemosus*), 93

T

Tackifier, 129–30
Tanks, 46–47, 72–73
Temperature, and fire ignition, 39
Thrift (*Armeria maritima*), 91
Topography
  and chaparral fires, 18
  homesites on slopes, 12–13
  impact of, 25, 38
  influence on wildfires, 7, 10–11
Tottentot fig, 76
Trailing gazania (*Gazania leucolaena*), 79, 81, 90
Trailing iceplant (*Lampranthus spectabilis*), 76
Trailing lantana (*Lantana montevidensis*), 87
Trailing South African daisy (*Osteopermum fruticosum*), 79, 81, 85
Tree canopy, 62, 67
Trees
  conifers, 93
  deciduous, 92
  planting on slopes, 130
  reforestation, 131–33
  spacing of, 61, 64, 66–68
  tree farms, 149
Tulip tree (*Liriodendron tulipfera*), 94

U

U.S. Fish and Wildlife Service, 26, 142
U.S. Forest Service, 131
University Cooperative Extension Service, 143

University of California Agricultural Publications, 143
Urban forests, 20–21
Urban–wildlife interface, 5, 25–26, 55–57, 135
USDA Soil Conservation Service, 46, 51
  services offered by, 118, 142

V

Valley oak (*Quercus lobata*), 93
Vegetation
  and fires, 18
  management of, 59
  and roadway safety, 27–28
Vents, 30, 111, 112
Vines, 78

W

Water, 43–54, 72
  access, 28–29, 48–50, 52–54
  emergency supplies, 44–48
  maintenance of, 104–105
  availability of, 24, 70
Well house, 49
White trailing iceplant (*Delosperma* 'Alba'), 76
Wildfires
  benefits of, 2, 10
  effects on soil, 120–21
  emotional impact of, 145–46
  history of, 2–3
  most common sources of, 40–42
  movement of, 10–11
Wildlife agencies, restrictions from, 26
Wild strawberry (*Fragaria chiloensis*), 81
Wind, 13, 17, 21, 38–39
Windows
  covering, 111, 112
  transmission of heat, 31
Wintercreeper, 80
Wooly thyme (*Thymus pseudolanuginosus*), 82
Wooly yarrow (*Achillea tomentosa*), 78, 80

Y

Yellow trailing iceplant (*Malephora luteola*), 77